Christians
and the
COMMON
GOOD

How Faith Intersects with Public Life

CHARLES E. GUTENSON

BrazosPress

a division of Baker Publishing Group
Grand Rapids, Michigan

Published by Brazos Press
a division of Baker Publishing Group
P.O. Box 6287, Grand Rapids, MI 49516-6287
www.brazospress.com

Printed in the United States of America

Library of Congress Cataloging-in-Publication Data
Gutenson, Charles E.
    Christians and the common good : how faith intersects with public life /
Charles E. Gutenson.
        p.   cm.
    Includes bibliographical references and index.
    ISBN 978-1-58743-287-3 (pbk.)
    1. Common good—Religious aspects—Christianity. 2. Common good—Biblical teaching. I. Title.
BR115.P7G87 2011
261.70973—dc22   2010046410

11   12   13   14   15   16   17   7 6 5 4 3 2 1

Dedicated to Mary Louise Miracle Gutenson
January 26, 1932–January 24, 2010

Contents

Foreword

JIM WALLIS

I have often said that God is personal but never private, and that the witness of the biblical prophets and Jesus must be recovered for our times and courageously applied to a whole range of moral and political issues. But what does it mean to use the content of what the Old Testament prophets, Jesus, and the New Testament writers had to say and apply it to our public commitments, our common life, and the social bonds we share in community?

Too often, we don't seriously study the Scriptures; it is much easier to just use God to justify our own politics. Yet if we really look into the biblical texts, we find a God who speaks about "politics" all the time—about what believing in God means in this world (not just the next one), about faith and public life (not just private piety), and about our responsibilities for the common good (not just for our own religious experience).

In *Christians and the Common Good*, Chuck Gutenson outlines some of the common ways we use (and misuse) the Bible. He then systematically lays out a more serious, disciplined, and holistic way to go about reading the Scriptures that studies the importance of context, the place of the overall biblical narrative, and how they apply to our contemporary situation. He proposes that the central question we must ask is, What does the Bible tell us about the nature of God? He then outlines a series of central beliefs about the being and nature of God.

The big "political" questions that face us ultimately have to do with how we are to live together in human community. As we examine what the Bible has to say about the nature of God, we can draw lessons that help us answer those questions. What does it tell us about how we are to live together? What in God's nature shows God's intention and priorities for how we are to live together for the common good of all? The heart of the book is a study of biblical vignettes that illustrate God's intentions and priorities for us and our society, and provide broad themes of what a community that pleases God would look like.

We must finally determine the relationship between God's agenda and human governance—what is the proper role of Christian faith in developing public policies, and what are the respective roles for government and the church? With all of this as the foundation, the book uses some examples of applying biblical study to specific issues, and suggesting which policy themes would best empower an agenda for the common good.

At this time in American history when people of faith across the political spectrum are engaging more in public policy and in politics, this is an ideal book for Sunday school classes, Bible study groups, and other discussion groups. I have been blessed to work closely with Chuck for the past several years at Sojourners, and I am thankful that he has brought together his substantial theological training and his public policy concerns in *Christians and the Common Good.* At a time when the relationship between faith and politics, the role of government, and the vocation of the church are all hotly contested issues, Chuck Gutenson's keen theological insights, deeply biblical approach, and clear political analysis will be a great help to us all.

Acknowledgments

I t is hard for me to imagine writing any book without serious support and encouragement on any one of a number of fronts—colleagues to brainstorm with and to critique your ideas, friends to urge you on, and family willing to bear the pensive periods that accompany thinking through difficult issues. In my case, thanks be to God, I had support in every one of these ways, and I want to take this opportunity to express my thanks—though, undoubtedly, I will overlook some. A number of colleagues participated in many, often passionate discussions over the topics addressed herein. These include my doctoral mentor, William J. Abraham; my dean at the time of writing the first draft, Joel Green; my teaching colleagues, Lawrence Wood, Virginia Todd Holeman, Mike Rinkiewich, and Michael Pasquarello; and my good friend, Will Samson. On later drafts, I benefited from various conversations with my Sojourners colleagues Jim Wallis and Duane Shank. At a point when I was not sure the project could go on, friendly and affirming encouragement from Brian McLaren was indispensable. To Heidi Thompson I owe thanks for some key structural changes I made early on; I am sure these made the final product much stronger than it would have been. My daughter, Sara Gutenson Monroe, has been a source of joy and inspiration from the day she was born to a degree far greater than she will ever know. And last, but hardly least, how can I say thank you enough to a wife and partner of over thirty years who was willing to follow a young man who felt the call to abandon a blossoming career in business because he felt "there had to be more than this"? Thanks, Bobbie!

In giving these thanks, however, I own the claims in this work as my own. May God grant you remembrance of all that is in alignment with his intentions and forgetfulness for all that is not.

Charles E. Gutenson

Introduction

I am sure you recall the old adage: religion and politics are two subjects to avoid in polite conversation. Well, the times have changed. Now it seems one can hardly discuss one without the other, even if mostly to criticize those who disagree. Those who are right of center characterize those who are left of center as "Godless liberals." Those left of center charge those who are right of center of having a penchant for "fundamentalism," if not theocracy—a government where the nation is ruled directly by God. (Of course, that this "direct rule" is to be carried out by those who happen to be the advocates of theocracy and their particular interpretation of God's will might legitimately raise eyebrows.) What has made these discussions more popular and at the same time more difficult? Perhaps it comes from a general loss of civility and our growing inability to live in peace with those who have commitments different from our own. Maybe these trends preclude the gentility of an earlier day. Or maybe we simply never really lived by the injunction to avoid politics and religion in polite conversation. Maybe this notion is a revisionist, wishful remembrance of our past. Who knows?

I grew up in what would today be characterized as a "fundamentalist" Christian tradition. Of course, for us to admit back then that we were fundamentalists was only an abstract theological observation. While we were comfortably fundamentalist in our Christian outlook, we had not yet been educated about the necessity of combining that religious commitment with political commitments. In fact, given that my fundamentalist church was located among the working class, I suspect that we were overwhelmingly populist in political outlook, which means that we would have mostly voted for Democratic candidates. I say "I suspect" because we rarely talked about political office, campaigns, and the like. We knew about the work of Martin Luther King Jr. and others who were engaged in the struggle for civil rights. However, that seemed like a faraway world that had little if anything to do with our everyday lives. And even though we realized that King's work was connected with the church in some way, it always seemed more political to us than religious. From time to time, however, I would read something about King or, say, something from the life of the early church, and a nagging suspicion would develop that there was more to being a Christian than I was aware—for example, that the life of faith had intimate connections with the struggle for justice, fairness, and so forth. Few if any Christians were around, however, to help resolve those nagging suspicions.

We certainly thought we were living in community (though not an intentional or monastic community). If someone had pushed us on the connections between what it means to be "in community" and what it means to be "political"—after all, to be political first and foremost means to be concerned about the lives that we share together in community—we *might* have understood. Unfortunately, in that day our focus on community was in the very provincial sense of the term—we were interested first and foremost in those things that concerned *us*. While we would have affirmed the biblical concern for the poor, we did not really see the obligation to provide for the physical needs of those who were not our immediate neighbors. We prayed for those on the other side of the world, but we did very little to ease their hunger, malnutrition, and disease. Once or twice a year we raised money to send missionaries to those faraway places, but that was to aid in the saving of their souls, not to care about their physical lives. "Political" was a term too loaded with worldliness for us to see that it had much connection with our daily Christian lives. We failed to see the profoundly political implications of the life of Jesus. In fact, if Jesus and politics were mentioned in the same breath, it was only to deny that Jesus was political at all. Following Jesus was a very private matter. It should not have been, for if we are following Jesus—if it is indeed Jesus we are following—the last thing it can be is a private matter.

Perhaps the biggest obstacle to our coming to see the political implications of Christianity was the extent to which our preaching and teaching were focused on individual salvation. The goal of every church service was to confront people with the choice to accept Christ as their personal Savior. While no one would have been so crass as to say so, we hardly knew what was left for them to do once that decision was made except to persuade others to accept Christ as their personal Savior also. I was frequently puzzled as I attempted to locate in Scripture this very narrow sense of "being saved"; I personally walked away from Scripture with the impression that conversion was merely a first step in a life of increasing conformity to the image of Christ. The almost exclusive focus on individual salvation through conversion wreaked havoc on our attention to discipleship. What was really the first step became the only step that really mattered. In the process, everything else we did to engage in service to those around us became an instrument of evangelism, and the recipients of our "largess" rarely missed that fact.

We had not yet come to the point at which obsession with gay marriage was such an issue—we just did not think about "them." I am sure that I came in contact with homosexual people from time to time, but I never really gave it much thought. Likewise, it is very likely that I knew people who had had abortions, but we never spoke of it. In pre–Roe v. Wade America, dangerous backroom abortions were a well-known "secret," but not one that most religious folks were particularly inclined to worry about. The church in which I grew up had not yet been confronted with the two issues that seem to be most frequently cited as reasons why Christians must become politically active and, further, why they must vote for a particular political party.

I am not so sure that our grasp of what constituted moral issues then was any broader than it is today. Rather, I suspect it was even narrower, for our attention to what it meant to live out a life of holiness was normally characterized negatively, that is, by the things we *did not* do. For example, there was a popular old saying that "Good Christian boys do not smoke, drink, or chew, or run around with girls that do." (As you can see, even in the way we framed the issues, we had not yet come to realize that sexism was an incipient problem.) It was a time when Christian faith was embodied by resisting the things we thought the worldly were inclined to do. One wonders if George Barna were doing his work then whether he would have found that, as today, there really was no difference between the way we lived our lives and the way non-Christians did. Such was my experience.

In the midst of this version of the Christian faith, I experienced a significant level of disquiet. What the Bible seemed to demand of followers of Jesus was far more radical than anything I was hearing. It did not make sense to me that the Prince of Peace would have supported the war in Vietnam. Likewise, it seemed hard to hold together the rather crass materialism that Christians seemed to increasingly embrace with the biblical command to deny ourselves and take up our crosses. I could not understand why the Bible seemed to reflect a God who cared so much for the poor, yet we so often tended to blame the poor for their own plight. In short, there were many disconnects between my life of faith and what it seemed to me Scripture taught about what the life of faith was supposed to be like.

I did not then fully realize the extent to which our basic failure to see the relationship between Christian faith and political engagement was at the root of many of these disconnects. If I had really allowed the biblical narratives to soak in, perhaps I would have seen that relationship. Jesus's challenges to the authority of Caesar, the possibility of the church embodying a different political economy in the world, and the reality that all powers have been appointed by God to serve God were notions that occasionally flitted around the margins of my consciousness. But I had no way to take them in and process them. It was a naïve day for a naïve boy in a naïve tradition. Some days I wish that naïveté had remained, but it did not. I was increasingly left alone to sort out the implications of Christian faith and its intersections with political life. In what follows, we will explore a number of issues that reside at those intersections. At the end, by the grace of God, perhaps we will be better able to understand what it means to be imitators of Christ in a much more holistic fashion than that naïve farm boy could have ever hoped.

1

Faith and Politics

Why, from a Christian perspective, should we think that economic justice is a concern for governments? Why not simply embrace a free market economy and let churches and private charities help with the marginalized? I suspect all of us have heard these questions. They are usually accompanied by claims that Jesus was apolitical and that he did not indicate that governments should be involved in care for "the least of these." These are popular ideas, but are they correct? Is it really the case that governments have no role to play in what might be broadly called a "kingdom agenda"? I believe these sentiments miss important aspects of biblical narratives, and in this book, we will explore the reasons for that belief.

If it were ever the case that we could separate faith from political models, it is certainly very difficult to do so today. Voter guides are regularly distributed in churches, some pastors feel emboldened enough to tell their parishioners what conclusions to draw and how to vote, and political themes often make their way into sermons. Some churches have taken the intertwining of church teaching and partisan politics so far as to skirt IRS rules, risking their tax-free status. The remarkable popularity of Jim Wallis's book *God's Politics* seems to demonstrate that many are hungry for serious engagement of the questions addressing the relationship between faith and politics.[1] This in turn has encouraged numerous authors from both the right and the left to join the conversation.[2]

Colleges and universities have invited authors such as Brian McLaren, Jim Wallis, and Shane Clairborne to speak or to teach courses developed around religious engagement with politics. Pollsters and sociologists seem ever creative in their ability to come up with new ways to assess this interest in the political habits and beliefs of religious folks. Numerous websites (often the wild and woolly world of blogs, Facebook, Twitter, etc.) have appeared in order to provide forums for the presentation of ideas and to foster discussion between those seeking solid ground for their theopolitical commitments. I suppose if one really tried one could find places where theology and politics are still held at arms' length. But those places are becoming less common.

One thing I find remarkable in the current theopolitical climate is how difficult it is to find treatments either by those on the political left or the political right that take seriously the founding text of the Christian faith—the Bible. In some cases people avoid the biblical texts outright. How many times have you heard people talk about what sorts of political positions Jesus would have undoubtedly supported but never bother to tell us what Jesus actually said? Or how many times have you heard someone make a claim about what Scripture says about some political position and then cite a biblical passage in support of it? Consider the claim that "Jesus was not political," which is usually supported with a passage such as Luke 20:25. In this case, once one examines the broader context of Luke 20, one can see that this passage does not actually support the claim.

I recently came across a statement by an organization opposed to legalizing abortion. The organization claimed rather strongly that "'God is pro-life' (Deut. 30:19)." I dutifully opened my Bible to the referenced passage only to find that the words "choose life" came at the end of Moses's address to the Israelites just before they were to enter the Promised Land. Moses had described to the people a set of instructions from God. He then said, in essence, if the people obeyed these instructions, they would live well in the land; if they disobeyed them, it would mean death. The command to choose life was Moses's way of saying, "I have given you God's instructions. God's instructions lead to life. So choose life! Be obedient!"

My point is not whether one can build a biblical case for or against abortion. Rather, I point out that this passage was cited simply because the catch phrase "choose life" was present, not because it had anything to do with abortion. Those reframing the passage clearly intended to trade on the fact that the phrase deployed by their organization was a phrase one could find in Scripture. One can find ever more egregious examples if one takes the time to look. However, when we as Christians abuse Scripture and apply it so poorly, we give the impression to all that we are not so much interested in taking Scripture seriously as we are interested in seeing how we can deploy it to score rhetorical points. In this case, a very small part of one verse was ripped from its surrounding context in order to appear to give divine sanction to a position the organization holds. If we are to engage in serious dialogue about the relationship between Christian faith and our political commitments, we must invest more energy in bringing Scripture to bear on them. We must attempt to understand what Scripture is actually saying rather than carelessly bending it to fit our political agendas. That does not mean, of course, that there will not continue to be debate about what given texts mean. But we should and must engage in a more serious treatment of biblical narratives.

Some would respond to this challenge by arguing that Scripture does not really say enough about politics for us to draw any particularly helpful conclusions about what sort of political life God intends. When this argument is put forward, it is often supplemented by an appeal to "statecraft"—the craft of forming and managing nation-states, a craft that often requires us to appeal to extrabiblical rationale. This does not render issues of statecraft irrelevant, but it invites us to critique them from a biblical perspective.

We should not so quickly conclude that Scripture cannot be mined for insights on theopolitical matters. The fact that they do not always say what we want them to say does not mean they have nothing to teach us. Any time we as Christians are tempted to move beyond Scripture in drawing conclusions on these complicated matters, we should recall 1 Corinthians 1:18–25:

> For the message about the cross is foolishness to those who are perishing, but to us who are being saved it is the power of God. For it is written,
>
> "I will destroy the wisdom of the wise,
>   and the discernment of the discerning I will thwart."
>
> Where is the one who is wise? Where is the scribe? Where is the debater of this age? Has not God made foolish the wisdom of the world? For since, in the wisdom of God, the world did not know God through wisdom, God decided, through the foolishness of our proclamation, to save those who believe. For Jews demand signs and Greeks desire wisdom, but we proclaim Christ crucified, a stumbling-block to Jews and foolishness to Gentiles, but to those who are the called, both Jews and Greeks, Christ the

power of God and the wisdom of God. For God's foolishness is wiser than human wisdom, and God's weakness is stronger than human strength.

I am not yet ready to draw any political conclusions from this passage. I cite it merely as a reminder as we proceed that, for us as Christians, no part of our lives escapes God's power displayed on the cross. Regarding the fact that this display of power is "foolishness to Gentiles" (who ever heard of displaying power through suffering?) and a "stumbling-block to Jews" (how could this character be the long awaited Messiah who was, after all, supposed to be a political leader who ousted the Romans?), I dare say the cross is too often foolish in both of those ways to us as well. Our need to look for extrabiblical rationale for deploying power in more conventional ways is but a symptom of our lack of faith and imagination. After all, who really wants to look weak and foolish? We live in a day in which strength and power rule and in which any sign of weakness is seen as giving too much credibility to our opponents. Surely we can agree that things have deteriorated too far when the call for diplomacy is so often dismissed as appeasement.

All this raises a very important question I will ask the reader to keep in mind as we proceed through our study. Are we, as Christians, genuinely able to embrace the overarching narrative of Scripture in such a way that it gains authority over us? If our best judgments incline us in one way but our best understanding of what God calls us to do leads us in another direction, which path will we follow? What if the life and teaching of Jesus really do turn our normal conceptions of power and strength upside down? Can we allow ourselves to be formed by the biblical narratives if they undermine common sense? If not, one has to wonder in what sense we would claim our positions to be Christian in the end. Perhaps the gospel really is far more radical than any of us are willing to admit. Where does the cross of Christ fit in our day-to-day practices in our communities? What does it mean to take up our crosses and follow Jesus, even in the political realm?

Again, perhaps the most significant problem in popular discussions of Christian ideas about politics and the role public institutions are to have in a kingdom agenda is the failure of those discussions to take Scripture with adequate seriousness. When these questions arise, people often appeal to a handful of common prooftexts. Romans 13, Luke 20 (and the parallel passages from the other Gospels), and John 18 are three such prooftexts. Romans 13 references "ruling authorities" and connects that authority with God. However, it is often read with very little attention to the surrounding context. In Luke 20, Jesus says we are to give Caesar's things to Caesar and God's things to God. But rarely do we hear what Jesus could have meant in light of either the immediate context of this particular chapter or the broader context of Jesus's teaching. The last passage, John 18, has Jesus affirming that his kingdom "is not of this world." Yet this passage cannot be read apart from the rest of Jesus's ministry or the later affirmation of the lordship of Jesus over all thrones and powers. While these passages have relevance for our attempts to grasp God's intentions for our lives together, they are not sufficient to warrant the antipolitical conclusions that are often drawn from them. We will have to expand our discussion far beyond these passages and attempt to understand the "bigger picture" of what God is doing before we can claim to have adequate information to draw conclusions. Throughout this book we will aim to see this bigger picture.

I believe that the proper starting point for identifying the sorts of policies that might serve a kingdom agenda is by attempting to discern God's intentions for common life. I do this by simply asking, "How does God intend for us to live together?" This is not an easy question to answer because it requires us to read the biblical narratives deeply. We must first seek to discover the sorts of characteristics that societies satisfying God's intentions should have. We must then examine policy options that might enable and empower societies to conform to the divine intent. This will require five distinct steps.

Discerning God's Intentions

First, we will have to examine the manner in which we read and understand Scripture. You will not have to read far into biblical commentaries to find points of disagreement as to what particular texts mean. There are several reasons for this. One is that some texts are very difficult to translate from the original languages. Another reason has to do with the basic presuppositions we bring to the Bible regarding how it is to be read. Do we read more to be formed by the narratives, or to extract universal principles that we can apply to all situations? Do we tend to read abstractly, or do we see the importance of the concrete situations within which each particular text is embedded? Do we interpret Scripture from an overarching holistic perspective? Or do we tend to search for prooftexts that deal with particular issues? To what extent do we read Scripture through a lens formed by the life and teachings of Jesus? These are all critically important questions, each of which requires careful attention before we can talk about the implications of biblical teaching for particular questions. We will consider these issues in chapter 2.

Second, we must not lose sight of the fact that Scripture is first and foremost about who God is and what God is like. This may sound shocking to some. Many of us approach Scripture primarily to find out how God wants us to live, and Scripture becomes primarily about what we are to do. But it is only by grasping God's character and nature that we begin to discern what God expects of us. In many places in Scripture, we are instructed to be imitators of God. However, if we are to imitate God, we must first know what God is like. Only then can we give serious attention to imitating God. We must approach Scripture realizing that it is the story of God's interaction with humanity, and this story constitutes the disclosure of God's nature. Chapter 3 will focus on this process, which in turn will provide insights into what it means to be called to be imitators of God.

The third step is to determine the implications of the divine nature for helping to discern a way of living together that satisfies God's expectations. The Christian tradition has consistently affirmed the triune nature of God. God is a community of persons living in perfect love. In order to think about God's intentions for our way of living together and the implications for our public lives and institutions, we will reflect on what it would mean to imitate God, who is a community. This is the subject of chapter 4.

The next step occurs in chapter 5. While it would take several books of this size to complete an exhaustive survey of the biblical narratives, we will examine a number of them. We will start with Genesis and progress through the Scriptures, stopping here and there to consider different places where God's intentions for how we are to live together are expressed. These "biblical vignettes" are not offered as prooftexts for the points I will be making. Rather, I intend for them to serve as data points that will allow us to draw preliminary conclusions about the way God intends for us to live together. We will consider specific commands that God gives at different times as well as places where God passes judgment on his people for failing to live up to his intentions. At some points, we will attempt to discern the reasons behind the commands that God gives. For example, it is not enough merely to observe that God commanded the observance of Years of Jubilee and Years of Release (Leviticus 25 and 27). In order to see what sorts of policies and institutions might serve a similar purpose in the twenty-first century, we must attempt to inquire about God's reasons for commanding these observances.

Only after we are able to round out our grasp of the divine nature, understand its implications for how we are to live together, and see how this is embodied in the different biblical vignettes will we be ready to ask the question of what sorts of public policies would encourage and empower the kingdom agenda we have been able to discern.[3] This approach is different from the one often undertaken to support particular views on the relationship between faith and politics. Too often studies of this nature have started with questions such as, what is the biblical role of government? Or, from a biblical perspective, should governments be involved in this or that particular kind of practice? I am arguing that these questions cannot be treated seriously apart from a more in-depth examination of Scripture. Chapters 2–5 set the stage for chapter 6, where we consider specific policies and institutions and reflect on how they might satisfy different aspects of God's intentions for how we are to live together. By proceeding in this fashion, we are not simply attempting to see what the Bible has to say about government. We consider the nature of government and public policy only as part of a broader attempt to understand how God has created us to live together. Forms of government or public policies should never be seen as ideological ends, but always as means to an end—in our case, the communal life that God intends for us.

It should come as no surprise that we will not come to a single answer about the sorts of public policies and/or institutions that will satisfy God's expectations. This is partly because we will never realize God's expectations perfectly. Any given proposal we might present will always be subject to improvement. Many different policies could satisfy God's expectations because God's expectations mostly relate to *outcomes*. In other words, we will come to see that God does not so much care whether we have this or that form of public institution. Instead, he is most concerned that certain things are accomplished, for example, that the poor and the marginalized are properly cared for and that the powerful are not left free to exploit the weak. These are aspects of our life together for which God, as we shall see, consistently expresses concern. Whether we accomplish this with a parliamentary system, a representative democracy, or some other system is very much secondary. We will consider possible structures and policies that will allow God's expectations to be accomplished, but recognize that these proposals are more illustrative than prescriptive. Once again, the goal is to enable and empower a way of being and living together that serves a kingdom agenda, an agenda preeminently focused upon human flourishing.

Challenges

It is worth reflecting briefly on the kinds of problems that have tended to stand in the way of better assessments of public policy from a Christian perspective. Unfortunately, given the complexities of public life and the wide-ranging expectations God has for us, there is a remarkable degree of temptation to simply ignore issues. If one believes that God is only really concerned with a couple of issues, it becomes easier to ignore others. But human life, particularly our common public life, is just too complicated for this kind of reductionist approach. Any genuinely Christian position on the role of public institutions and policies will have to reckon with the fact that so many (too many, both globally and nationally) are in poverty, that proper health care is increasingly difficult to obtain, and that we too eagerly and too often find reasons to go to war. Additionally, we will have to articulate a consistent agenda that affirms the sanctity of life, finds ways to encourage and empower families to flourish, and develops strategies for tending to the good creation with which God has entrusted us. I could go on, but the point is evident: there is a wide range of moral issues to which Christians must attend, and the popular tendency to engage in reductionism to make the problems seem simpler can no longer be tolerated.

This is not to say, of course, that public institutions and policies are the centerpieces of the solution to each issue. We must recognize, however, that public policies and institutions (either affirmatively by presence or negatively by absence) affect these and other issues profoundly. Further, since they affect our ability to live out God's intentions for us, specific public policies and insitutions are important and relevant for Christians who are reflecting on the relationship between faith and politics.

When the church allows itself to be distracted from attending to the wider range of theopolitical issues, when it allows itself to give credence to a reductionist moral agenda, it becomes increasingly unable to provide an alternative to "business as usual" in the culture. By focusing narrowly on such issues as abortion and homosexuality, for example, the church loses its ability to critique so many of the other problems that face our world today. Worse, it puts itself in a position of appearing to not take the teachings of its own Scriptures (and founder!) seriously, thus ultimately undermining its own authority and credibility. In fact, the church begins to appear as little more than a social club with particular practices it tends to avoid, with little substantive difference between its members and the culture at large.

In several of his works, George Barna points out just how little difference there is between those who claim to be born-again Christians and those who do not claim to be Christians.[4] In fact, he often finds that non-Christians are more generous in giving to the poor, are about equally as likely to have engaged in extra-marital sex, and that Christians are, sadly, more likely to have had divorces than non-Christians. And the rampant materialism of our culture is no more apparent than in the parking lots of most large churches on Sunday mornings. Quite simply, a major reason for the increasing irrelevance of the church for today's culture is its inability both to envision and to demand an alternative way of being in the world. Why bother with church when it has come to understand Christian faith as little more than an addendum to an otherwise secular dream of the good life? This secular dream is precisely what the church should be providing an alternative to, not baptizing and bringing inside its own life. For when we bring inside that dream, we bring with it the dysfunctions it carries. Barna found, for example, that the more conservative the church, the higher was the divorce rate. I am not suggesting there can be no proper basis for divorce. However, you would expect those who give loudest lip service to the notion of family values would be able to embody different priorities.

As Jim Wallis notes in his book *God's Politics*, one of the indications of the depth of the problem is that Jesus has come to be so strongly associated with positions that promote war and wealth and neglect the poor. In short, how did Jesus come to be aligned with so much in contemporary American politics that seems so at odds with Jesus's own teachings? Could we, for example, go to the Gospels, read carefully through Jesus's words, and conclude that the popular American picture of Jesus is consistent with Scripture? For many, the pictures are simply too divergent to make sense. It is just this disconnect that has caused many to take a step back, to reflect on the extent to which the Jesus they follow has been corrupted, and to ask what they might do about it. In some cases, the dissonance has been so great that the disillusioned have walked away from faith altogether. In the course of this book, we will have opportunity to work through these points in an effort to restore our footing to more solid ground. To the question at hand, we shall see that some of the primary reasons that so much of theopolitical discourse in the United States is off track include such things as biblical illiteracy and the failure to appreciate the importance of imitating Jesus.

Just how much are these problems directly related to political matters? It is often difficult to determine cause and effect. Is our understanding of Christian theology flawed, driving us to faulty political conclusions? Or is our understanding of politics flawed, driving us to faulty theological conclusions? The matter does not sort out quite so simply. Our theological and political errors are mutually reinforcing each other, and both have to be dragged out into the light for serious critique. One of the most significant issues facing both the political and the theological sides is the extent to which we have come to embrace power as the means to accomplish our ends. The gospel, however, describes us as a powerless people—or perhaps better, a people who embrace the power of the cross.

The power of self-sacrifice for the sake of others is at the core of the gospel and at the core of what it means to be followers of Jesus. As Steve Chalke once said to me, "The Christian life is all about winning by living in ways that look like you are losing."[5] Unfortunately, in our contemporary setting Christians on both the political left and right have been too willing to trade the power of the cross for a share in political power—and the attendant access to the inner workings of government. While we must be concerned for public policies and institutions to be structured in ways that serve a kingdom agenda (which aims for the flourishing of all, Christian or not), too often we cross the line to embracing political power as a means of enforcing a kingdom morality. These are very different things.

The attraction of power is both subtle and enticing. In their book *Blinded by Might*, Cal Thomas and Ed Dobson explore the ease with which political power entices us to think we can bring the kingdom by wielding power.[6] First, we think that if we stand firm for our principles, God will reward us with the political power to accomplish great things for the kingdom. Then we find that things are not so simple, that it will require compromise in order to accomplish those great things. So we make the compromises, rationalizing that they are, after all, insignificant compared to the good to be gained. Next, we find ourselves needing to defend the minor transgressions that seem so easily to follow those in positions of power. We again rationalize by arguing that the good to be gained offsets the unfortunate circumstances we find ourselves in. And so it continues, until we have so thoroughly compromised ourselves that we are actually only clinging to power for power's sake. We try to cover over our perversity with a veneer of Christian rhetoric for a time, but it quickly runs thin. People come to see the corruption, and the good we had hoped to do ends up being destructive to the kingdom. It is with good reason that the old adage claims that power corrupts, and that absolute power corrupts absolutely.

In the course of this chapter, we have laid out an agenda for the rest of the book. The next several chapters focus on how one reads and appropriates Scripture so as to be able to draw sound theopolitical conclusions about the sorts of public policies and institutions that will serve a kingdom agenda and lead to human flourishing. Along the way, we will take up the challenges to thinking rightly about the issues that we have identified in this chapter. It is my hope that as we work through this material, we might come to realize the importance of the affirmation that "God is not a Republican or a Democrat,"[7] but that both Republicans and Democrats may, however imperfectly, serve God's kingdom by grasping more fully the breadth and depth of moral issues that Christians are called to address in our contemporary world, and by coming to hold theopolitical commitments that are Christian first and political second.

2

Reading Scripture

It was a hot, humid evening in early August, and the small church in which I grew up was well into a two-week series of evangelistic services we called our "fall revival." The evangelist was delivering an obligatory sermon on hell, having prepared the way on previous nights by reminding us of all the unsavory character traits we possessed and how badly God hated them. Coincidentally, the air conditioning system was not working on this particular night. Combined with the miserably hot August weather, this gave a disquieting realism to the evangelist's preaching. He began by apologizing for having to speak to us on such a disturbing subject, much like a doctor who apologizes for the pain about to be caused by the life-saving measures he plans to undertake. "Jesus spoke of hell more often than of heaven," he assured us, "which means that though there is a heaven to be gained, there is a very real hell to be avoided." He did not pause to examine the contrast in the treatment of heaven and hell in Jesus's preaching. But this was neither here nor there. As the preacher, he was God's appointed man for the hour, which made him the authority on such matters. We dared not question or challenge his claims. To do so would not have been merely disrespectful to our evangelist but also a profound expression of a lack of faith in God's Spirit to speak through his chosen vessel. We sat back in nervous anticipation though we knew the general contours of what was to come.

The central text for that evening was Luke 12:1–5, with a particular emphasis on verses 4 and 5. In these verses, we are enjoined not to fear those who might only kill our physical bodies but instead fear the one who also has authority to cast us into hell. Any of us who did not respond to the evangelist's call to be saved would risk such a fate.

If we thought that this initial foray into the Bible through appeal to Luke 5 was the end of the evening's mining of God's Word, we were mistaken. The evangelist displayed a dazzling grasp of the Bible, and his ability to piece together a wide variety of texts into a message reinforcing his central theme was nothing short of stunning. In a nutshell, the sermon moved along the following lines:

> Brothers and sisters, Paul tells us that the wages of sin are death, but that the gift of God is eternal life [Rom. 6:23]. Salvation is a gift of God, a most precious gift, and there is nothing we can do to deserve it. Ephesians 2:8–9 tell us "for by grace you have been saved through faith," and this is not your own doing; it is the gift of God—not the results of works, so that no one may boast. How is it that we come to receive this gift? Jesus tells us that those whom the Son has set free are free indeed [John 8:36]. And how is it that the Son sets us free? By our putting faith in him. As we are told, if you confess with your lips that Jesus is Lord and believe in your heart that God raised him from the dead, you will be saved [Rom. 10:9].

So there we had it: an element of fear (specifically, the fear that God would cast us into hell), the unquestioned authority of the one making these claims (our evangelist), the appropriation of a variety of texts from the Bible, God's own authoritative word on these matters (represented by those appeals to Scripture), and the fortuitous cooperation of the weather to boot. I was too young to realize it at the time, but the factors had conspired against me, and there was no reasonable hope of actually hearing whatever subtleties God might have wished to convey.

At the end of the service, those factors had an effect. The altar of our little church was filled with new converts (or old converts rededicating themselves anew to avoiding hell). The evangelist beamed with, well, not pride, but perhaps satisfaction that "God's Word" had been so effective. But had it? If one had made a visit to the community prior to the "revival" and then revisited a scant two or three months afterward, one would have noticed little if any discernible difference in the behavior of that night's converts. How can we make sense of this? If it were God's Word being put before us that night, how could the long-term results be so inconsequential? Were there problems, after all, with the preacher's appropriation of Scripture? Of course, we were told that if pre- and post-conversion behavior were the same, it was the result of our perversity and in no way related to the evangelist's preaching style. But is this a valid assessment?

Being a firm believer in the claim that the Bible teaches a basic message of salvation through faith, I am particularly distressed to see that message trivialized into sermons that emphasize simply avoiding hell. Let us consider what was missing from this particular sermon in attempt to understand how such trivialization occurs. First, the sermon affirmed that humanity stands in need of restoration to healthy relationship with God, something the vast majority of Christians would readily affirm. However, the

sermon never really attempted to define what might constitute a
biblical sense of "salvation"—rich and varied, touching all aspects
of human existence. In place of that more careful examination was
what we could characterize as nothing more than an exhortation
to avoid hell. This vastly misrepresents the biblical picture of salvation as one of healing and wholeness—dangerously so, in fact.

As a side note, it is worth reflecting on the extent to which such
a reduced concept of salvation contributes to a remarkably low
level of commitment to discipleship. The push from the beginning
was to get everyone "converted"; there was very little follow-up
education, formal or informal, aimed at helping people understand
what it means to be a follower of Jesus. This in turn contributed
to the failure of "conversion" to result in lasting change. How
can you be faithful to following Jesus when the depths of what
it means to follow Jesus are never plumbed?

Second, each of these particular passages was pulled out of its
surrounding context and treated as if it were a short, pithy saying unconnected with any of the surrounding narrative. Thus it
could be deployed willy-nilly. For example, what exactly is Paul
getting at with his reference to the "wages of sin" and the "gift
of God"? How do these phrases function within the particular
letter in which they appear? When Paul speaks of being "saved
by grace through faith," what problem is he engaging? What
does he mean to affirm about the relation between faith, grace,
and salvation? And why does he seemingly denigrate the importance of works? James seems to have a rather different, or at least
substantially more nuanced, take on all this. How is this tension
to be understood?

When Jesus speaks of making us "free," what does he mean?
Does he really primarily mean "free from hell"? Or does this freedom run much deeper, perhaps having something to do with what
it means to be saved and to live a saved life in the world? Finally,

what depth and nuance must we consider when we reflect on the claim that a particular confession puts us into a saved relationship with God? Or does this miss the whole point? We never found out from our evangelist. While I am sure he was a sincere and devout person, he simply never engaged these questions. Instead, he treated Scripture as something we were all supposed to know like the backs of our hands, and he assumed that we all shared his presuppositions about how it was to be read.

Third and finally, this way of treating Scripture set an example for the rest of us. We came to think that we could mine Scripture for little tidbits that would fit a particular agenda we might have. We were never shown the importance of appropriating the Bible holistically, of taking care to consider each and every part within its own context, of being comfortable with the tensions that we inevitably encounter. One need only consider the haphazard way Scripture is often appropriated on both the right and the left to see that my experience was hardly unique. Is there a better and more serious way to appropriate Scripture? There is, and it is as old as the church itself.

Before we turn to that better way, however, let me make a couple of observations about how this story relates to our attempts to discern God's intentions for public policies and institutions. First, just as this evangelist took little pieces of verses from different places to try to build his case, so too do those seeking to discern the divine intent for public life. This approach gives an inadequate view of salvation, and it leads to an inadequate view of theopolitical issues as well. (In fact, it almost always leads to an inadequate few of virtually any issue.) Second, the tendency to focus so narrowly on individual salvation rather than the communal nature of salvation naturally leads us away from political concerns. Politics is about the life of the community, how communities are to be formed and structured. Individualistic conceptions of salvation fail, as we would expect, to deal adequately with the subtle nuances and complexities of public life.

We have already observed that discussions about the relationship between faith and politics have centered too narrowly on a relatively small set of texts. Appeals are most frequently made to these particular texts on the basis of their fairly explicit references to civil authority. A person could easily consult a biblical index or concordance for certain key words or phrases. Once the passages with these words and phrases have been located, they feel they now have the raw materials for forging a biblical position on the questions at hand. Of course, the fundamental problem here is the failure to recognize that this way of searching Scripture is just too narrow. Let us take a look at a few passages and suggest some ways in which the use of these references might be improved. Our examination is not intended to be exhaustive but rather identifies a few representative cases in order to flesh out a more holistic way of reading and interpreting Scripture. We will consider the passages we noted in the introduction: Romans 13 (something of a classic text on governmental authority), Luke 20 (and the parallels in the other Gospels), and John 18 (often cited to claim that Jesus was not political).

Romans 13

The passage perhaps most frequently referenced on these matters is Romans 13:1–7, which reads as follows:

> Let every person be subject to the governing authorities; for there
> is no authority except from God, and those authorities that exist
> have been instituted by God. Therefore whoever resists authority
> resists what God has appointed, and those who resist will incur

judgment. For rulers are not a terror to good conduct, but to bad. Do you wish to have no fear of the authority? Then do what is good, and you will receive its approval; for it is God's servant for your good. But if you do what is wrong, you should be afraid, for the authority does not bear the sword in vain! It is the servant of God to execute wrath on the wrongdoer. Therefore one must be subject, not only because of wrath but also because of conscience. For the same reason you also pay taxes, for the authorities are God's servants, busy with this very thing. Pay to all what is due them—taxes to whom taxes are due, revenue to whom revenue is due, respect to whom respect is due, honor to whom honor is due.

Appeal to this passage is often made in attempt to justify a minimalist view of government, a view that says governments are to simply restrain evil and promote the good. According to this interpretation, governments are not to be involved with issues of economic justice and other sociopolitical matters. Readers who interpret this passage in such a minimalist way fail to see that matters of economic and social justice are moral issues also, that is, good must be promoted and evil restrained. Thus one has to wonder whether this particular interpretation is even internally consistent. But there are other problems as well.

Appealing to this passage is not necessarily wrong. It provides an important part of the overall biblical narrative regarding the place God intends ruling authorities in our societies to occupy. For example, it seems to convey a very strong view of governmental authority as ordained and established by God. After all, it says that we should obey the governing authorities primarily because they are put in place by God. However, appealing to these verses without putting them into the broader context of Scripture misses much.

Consider how the authority and power of the state is relativized when we remember that the writer of this passage, the apostle

Paul, was executed as an enemy of the state. Whatever Paul says here about governmental authority has to be balanced against the reality that Paul himself did not take the words "whoever resists authority resists what God has appointed" to be unconditional. He himself refused to make the civil ruler's authority absolute *even if* he affirmed all authorities as ordained by God. Consequently, he openly disobeyed the law to the point of execution. How does this change our appropriation of this text? For one thing, it rules out reading this portion of Romans 13 either too literally or too uncritically. And it means that our reading of the biblical texts in attempt to discern God's intent for our common life is going to require a good deal more thoughtfulness than merely "index shopping" for key prooftexts.

Regarding the context of Romans 13, consider Romans 12, where Paul lays out God's vision for what common life should look like. We are enjoined to think of others more highly than ourselves, to welcome the stranger, and to live peaceably with all. The chapter concludes by telling us that the standard for loving others is loving our enemies—a hard standard to live up to. But how often have you heard any reference to Romans 12 in discussions of Romans 13?

Some might argue that Romans 12 is addressed specifically to those who are already Christian believers. However, they will often then erroneously conclude that because not all are Christians, these commands have no place in considering what our common public lives should look like. I think this line of reasoning is mistaken. John Howard Yoder captures the reason in the following passage, which builds on the work of Karl Barth:

> The calling of the people of God is thus no different from the calling of all humanity. The difference between the human community as a whole and the faith community is a matter of aware-

ness or knowledge or commitment or celebration, but not of ultimate human destiny. *What believers are called to is no different from what all humanity is called to.* That Jesus Christ is Lord is a statement not about my inner piety or my intellect or ideas but about the cosmos. Thus the fact that the rest of the world does not yet see or know or acknowledge that destiny to which it is called is not a reason for us to posit or to broker some wider or thinner vision, some lower common denominator or halfway meeting point, in order to make the world's divine destination ... more acceptable or more accessible. The challenge to the faith community should not be to dilute or filter or translate its witness, so that the "public" community can handle it without believing, but so to purify and clarify and exemplify it that the world can perceive it to be good news without having to learn a foreign language.... If the community were to imagine that the reach of the sanctification of humanity accomplished in Jesus Christ were restricted to itself and the ingathering of believers, that it did not have corresponding effects *extra muros eclesiae* ["outside the walls of the church"], it would be in flat contradiction to its confession of its Lord.[1]

While Christians should perhaps be more aware or more empowered through God's Spirit to live as God intends, God's intentions are not different for the non-Christian community and the Christian community. The goals of our shared common life that conform to God's intentions are universal and not limited to the Christian community because God wills and desires the flourishing of all his creation. We can thus argue from passages such as Romans 12 in order to develop a bigger picture of God's intentions, which is relevant to understanding Romans 13.

If Romans 12 provides some insight into the life God intends for us, we will have to ask ourselves the question, What public policies and institutions help serve this vision? I am not claiming that the role of public policies and institutions is to legislate or forcibly enact the vision of Romans 12. Rather, whatever form these take, they are to serve that vision in some way—at least by encouraging and empowering it. Romans 13, when adequately considered with Romans 12 (and Scripture more broadly), does indeed provide help in our discernment of God's expectations for our shared, common lives. We must avoid making Romans 13 say more than it does about these matters, but we must also avoid judging it to be entirely irrelevant.

Luke 20:20–25

The next passage often mentioned is Luke 20 (and the parallels in Matthew and Mark).

> So they watched him and sent spies who pretended to be honest, in order to trap him by what he said, so as to hand him over to the jurisdiction and authority of the governor. So they asked him, "Teacher, we know that you are right in what you say and teach, and you show deference to no one, but teach the way of God in accordance with truth. Is it lawful for us to pay taxes to the emperor, or not?" But he perceived their craftiness and said to them, "Show me a denarius. Whose head and whose title does it bear?" They said, "The emperor's." He said to them, "Then give to the emperor the things that are the emperor's, and to God the things that are God's." And they were not able in the presence of the people to trap him by what he said; and being amazed by his answer, they became silent.

On the face of every coin was the emperor's likeness with wording affirming his divinity. For some, even using the Roman coins was tantamount to idolatry. If Jesus answers that they should pay the tax, the religious leaders could have seen this as breaking

Jewish law. Further, they are counting on a "yes" answer being unpopular with the people who view the Romans as the bad guys. But if he says that the tax should not be paid, then Jesus ends up in trouble with the Romans, for he would be encouraging the violation of Roman law. The questioners think they have him on the horns of a dilemma. Jesus, however, averts the snare by saying they should give to Caesar the things that are Caesar's and to God the things that are God's. For those who use this passage as a guide for the relationship between believers and civil government, Jesus's answer is often used to justify a division of realms: some things belong to the civil government while other things belong to God. But is this a reasonable interpretation of what Jesus is saying?

First, we have to set this interaction between Jesus and the religious leaders in its broader context. Specifically, the religious leaders are engaging in trickery to try to get back at Jesus for his implicit criticism of them in the parable of the wicked tenants (Luke 20:9–19). Nothing in the context suggests that Jesus is intending to give guidance on questions dealing with how Christians should view public institutions or civil government. Rather, we have every reason to think the primary point has to do with the hostile questioning from his interlocutors. We must be cautious about concluding too much by reading more into the story than it will bear.

Second, and perhaps more important, we have to seriously consider the possibility that Jesus is speaking with irony. If we take the overall context and direction of Jesus's ministry into consideration, does it really allow us to think that Jesus divided the world into two realms, only one of which is God's? Does God dismiss a "part" of the world? A much more consistent view would be one that understands what Jesus says here ironically. For Jesus, it is unimaginable that any aspect of human life extends beyond God's active involvement and lordship. Nothing in the immediate context leads us to believe that Jesus intends in this passage to deal with the role of civil governments in realizing God's intentions. Jesus's "two kingdoms" language is intended to sidestep the traps laid by the question. Consequently, this passage gives us little or no helpful information in determining what God intends regarding public policies and institutions.

John 18:33–37

One often hears John 18:33–37 cited to prove that Jesus did not understand his ministry to be political—or at least not political from the perspective of earthly kingdoms.

> Then Pilate entered the headquarters again, summoned Jesus, and asked him, "Are you the King of the Jews?" Jesus answered, "Do you ask this on your own, or did others tell you about me?" Pilate replied, "I am not a Jew, am I? Your own nation and the chief priests have handed you over to me. What have you done?" Jesus answered, "My kingdom is not from this world. If my kingdom were from this world, my followers would be fighting to keep me from being handed over to the Jews. But as it is, my kingdom is not from here." Pilate asked him, "So you are a king?" Jesus answered, "You say that I am a king. . . ."

What does Jesus mean when he says that his kingdom is not "of this world"? He goes on to affirm Pilate's reference to him as a king. Does this mean that Jesus is willing to accept the term as long as we realize that it is not to be applied to earthly kingdoms?

Rather than engaging in a lengthy examination of the finer nuances of this particular passage, let us make two quick observations. First, as those familiar with Scripture already know, God gives instructions about the form and content of our shared, common life in numerous places. We will examine several of these in a later chapter. God (and hence Jesus) cares very much about how we live with each other. Second, Scripture is clear that the affirmation "Jesus is Lord" is a statement about the lordship of Christ over all the created order. In some sense, Jesus's kingdom is in this world. It may be true that Jesus's kingdom is not *of* this world in the sense that it does not have its origins here. But because Jesus is Lord of all, his reign extends to this world and shapes and forms our lives together. As we continue our study, we will have to consider how these affirmations that seem to rest in tension are to be understood. For now, we simply observe that the overall shape of the biblical stories simply will not let us conclude from this single passage that Jesus means to deny the political implications of his life and ministry. N. T. Wright comments that it would have been strange indeed for a first-century Jew to have missed the profoundly political impact of Jesus's teachings.[2]

We could examine other passages, but since our focus for the moment is how one is to read and apply Scripture, let us stop to see what broader conclusions we might draw from these examples. In each case, the common interpretations suffer from a shared error, namely, the passage is too quickly applied directly to theopolitical questions. There is a lack of attention both to context (what is the overall passage addressing?) and nuance (how might this look in a different context?). The consequence is a too facile move from text to contemporary world. We should be very cautious in moving from biblical text to conclusions about how they can and ought to be applied to particular issues in our contemporary, very different setting. For example, one might read the passages from the Old Testament regarding Years of Jubilee and Years of Release and then too quickly move to suggest that contemporary economies must have these features. A more helpful way to look at such passages would be to ask a series of questions. First, we might ask, what is the underlying problem or opportunity that God is dealing with in giving this command to the people of that particular time? Second, do similar problems or opportunities face us in our contemporary setting? Third, how might God's concern for these problems or opportunities be embodied in today's world? Finally, what role might public policies and institutions play in helping to resolve these problems or taking advantage of these opportunities? In this way we both take Scripture seriously and attend to the contextual difference between our time and the time in which the text was written. Let us take the lessons we learned from our brief interaction with the three above passages and develop some guidelines for how we might read Scripture in a way that avoids common errors.

Reading Scripture: Guideline 1

While this is not a book about biblical hermeneutics, we can identify some straightforward guidelines to help us avoid some common errors. Let us consider four. First, one simply cannot read passages, verses, or pieces of verses as if they are unrelated to surrounding material. Nor can they be rightly interpreted without considering their places in the overarching biblical narrative. By overlooking the relevant contextual issues, there is a high degree of likelihood that we will miss the intent of the passage, and we will be much more likely to misuse it.

All of us have read material intending to answer questions about how the Bible treats this or that issue. Our goal, rightly, is to understand God's view of the matter. However, we must first see how the passage fits into the bigger picture of Scripture. For example, I have had students who attempt to justify modern warfare by appealing to Hebrews 13:8, which says, "Jesus Christ is the same yesterday and today and forever." First, they misquote the passage as saying "*God* is the same yesterday and today and forever," a subtle but important difference. Then they argue, "Since God allowed war in the Old Testament and since God never changes, we can conclude that God allows war today." One problem, of course, is that many things change from the Old to New Testaments. For example, during the Old Testament, animal sacrifice was practiced for atonement. The life of Jesus changed all that and, I would suggest, a whole lot more. The simplistic interpretation that leads us to conclude that nothing changes misses too much from the overall story. Whatever the writer of Hebrews is intending to affirm with this passage, it can not be stripped from its context and applied in this manner.

When we fail to read passages in their contexts, we often fall prey either to what I call the "pile-up-the-verses" approach or to the "insert-Bible-verse-here" approach. In the former, we do a search for key words or phrases. Once a list of passages with those key words or phrases is identified, we pile up the passages based on how they seem to deal with the issue at hand. The "most biblical" idea is the one with the biggest pile. In the latter approach, we don't take the time to pile up the verses but rather merely look for a single verse or passage that makes the point we want to make. We assemble our arguments first, leaving places to come back and find verses to insert. It gets the relationship between the positions we hold and the Bible backward; it attempts to find in the Bible support for a position we have already come to on other grounds.

Neither of these approaches does justice to Scripture's place in our lives. Sometimes the most insightful passages are those which, on first glance, may not even appear to be about the issue we are considering. Even if we do find all the various passages that deal with a given subject, we must come to realize that all passages require serious attention whether in support of or against our positions. As a wise man once said to me, all the Bible is Scripture—even the verses whose implications I do not like. Prooftexting, in all its forms, must be avoided like the plague.

Reading Scripture: Guideline 2

Second, and expanding on the importance of the first point, we all should commit to memory the three letters *c*, *i*, and *e*: *context is everything*. Everything in life exists in some particular context. Events and truth claims cannot be divorced from the contexts that give them meaning. Consider a speaker who says, "George was saved last night." If we know that the speaker is an evangelist or a preacher within a particular tradition, we might conclude that he was telling us about George's response to the gospel. On the other hand, if we know the speaker is an emergency medical technician, we would conclude something entirely different, for example, that George had been rescued from some sort of emergency situation. Context provides us with invaluable information without which we could not properly interpret the statement.

It is critical that we see how a particular passage of Scripture fits into the story Scripture is telling. Broadly speaking, there are at least two different levels for which context needs to be considered: (1) the immediately surrounding texts and (2) the context of the overarching biblical story. Let us reconsider the example of Luke 20, the passage where Jesus says to render to Caesar what is Caesar's and to God what is God's. Nothing in the immediate context suggests that this is intended to be an answer to the question about public policies or institutions, and it is exceedingly hard to imagine that Jesus intends to imply that there is some realm that is not God's. Instead, we have to see Jesus as affirming that all creation (secular, religious, or otherwise) belongs to God. His response is ironic. When we couple the immediate and the broader context, we can see that this popular prooftext really has nothing particularly helpful to say about the relationship between Christian faith and public institutions. Prooftexting is a common error easily solved by considering the context of Scripture.

Reading Scripture: Guideline 3

Third, a common question that we face in seeking to apply Scriptures is whether we can move directly from scriptural claims to applying them to our contemporary world. As we have seen, the answer is no. The sociocultural distance between us and the time when the biblical texts were written makes a simple move directly from a biblical text to a contemporary application impossible. We have to move more indirectly, in a way that takes into account that sociocultural distance while at the same time not allowing that distance to silence Scripture's voice to us today. In other words, one cannot simply observe the laws of Jubilee given by God in Leviticus 25 and then conclude that we are to include laws requiring the observance of Jubilee in contemporary economies.

But we must take the biblical texts relating to laws of Jubilee seriously. How do we do that while avoiding direct application? I suggest asking four questions:

1. Why did God command this? That is, what opportunities or challenges was God trying to enable or prevent?
2. Are there current, comparable opportunities or challenges?
3. What would satisfy God's intentions in our contemporary world?
4. What role, if any, do civil institutions have to play?

This allows us to take the biblical evidence seriously while also taking into account the contemporary situation. So, for example, if we were to take these steps with respect to the laws of Jubilee, one might conclude that God's reason for giving this command was to prevent the rise of a permanently dispossessed class of people. In fact, one might take the Years of Jubilee as well as the Years of Release (all debts were to be cancelled every seventh year; Deuteronomy 15) and see them as God's plan for making sure that there are no poor among his people. This periodic economic "re-leveling" helped to avoid the accumulation of great wealth in the hands of a few, which far too often results in great poverty for others. The underlying challenge that God was intending to resolve by establishing Years of Jubilee and Years of Release was an economic stratification of his people in which some had more than plenty while others had too little.

We need not pause long on the second question, for the problem of economic stratification and poverty has existed in all cultures at all times. We can easily conclude that the same challenges and opportunities that faced the ancient Israelites also face our culture today.

We can be similarly brief with regard to the third question: God's intention for his people is that everyone should have enough. One might consider, for example, 2 Corinthians 8:15, where Paul observes that "the one who had much did not have too much, and the one who had little did not have too little." I cite this passage not as a prooftext but rather as an example of the consistent theme of Scripture that God intends, as we noted above, for no one to be poor. We too face the question of how we avoid the economic stratification that inevitably results in too little for too many of God's children.

This brings us to the place where we must rightly begin to reflect on the variety of ways in which God's intention might be served. We should not expect that there is only one way in which this goal can be accomplished. There will be a good deal of ideological debate, but once we are clear on the goal, working toward the best solution should simply be a matter of trial and error. Of course, our idea of what constitutes "too much" for me and "too little" for them is often skewed by our own selfishness. Without constant recognition of the consistent biblical theme to put others' interests over our own, we too easily tilt the playing field in our own favor. With these things in mind, we must reflect upon the socioeconomic conditions of our own cultures, and ask how we might realize God's intention that there not be some with too much and others with too little in our contemporary setting. There are a number of possible policy positions one might take on this question, and we shall consider some later in chapter 6. Taking the time required to address these four questions makes our application of Scripture a bit more complicated than engaging in direct application, but it helps us to avoid missing the genuine intent God had in mind.

Reading Scripture: Guideline 4

This brings us to our last interpretive guideline. If we are to avoid prooftexting and come to see Scripture more holistically, we must learn to see the grand, overarching narrative of Scripture. Rather than seeing the Bible as a collection of sixty-six rather loosely connected books (or more, depending on your tradition), we need to see that the Bible is the *one story* of God's interaction with creation. As with all good narratives, Scripture starts somewhere, is going somewhere, and progressively reveals its contents. Learning to understand Scripture in this way requires patience and serious engagement, but the payoff is well worth it. We must learn to ask questions such as, Where is God's story going? What are the obstacles that must be overcome along the way? What is God up to now? How do we align ourselves with God's activity in the world? As we begin to better understand the big picture, we will become better at seeing how the various passages serve the bigger story, and we will become better at drawing conclusions about God's intentions for us. Because this point is of such significance, let us turn our attention in more detail to what it means to read the Bible both as Scripture and as narrative.[3]

To start with, what does it mean to say that one reads the Bible "as Scripture"? We often use the terms somewhat interchangeably, but it is worth reflecting on what this means.

First, to treat a particular text or set of texts as Scripture is to recognize that they have an authority that is ultimately derived from God. Historically, the church has understood this in different ways, never settling on a single definition of what it means to say that God has given us the Scriptures. Each definition, however, assigns an important level of authority to the claims made in the scriptural texts.

Second, to treat the Bible as Scripture is to recognize that this particular set of texts exercises authority *over us* in some sense. This has also been taken differently within the Christian tradition, but to accept the Bible as Scripture is to accept that the Bible, properly understood, conveys both God's nature to us and, derivatively, his expectations for our lives.

Third, to treat the Bible as Scripture is to place the biblical texts at the center of the life of faith in such a way that we realize and affirm the importance of discerning what they have to say about God and his relationship with creation. It follows, then, that we should be concerned to read the Bible rightly and to invest ourselves in regular, formative engagement with the biblical texts.

Having said something of what it means to read the Bible as Scripture, it is also important to be clear on what it does not mean. To treat the Bible as Scripture is not to say that we must read the biblical texts literally. While some argue that this is the only way to take Scripture seriously, I argue that we take Scripture seriously only when we read it as God intends. In our everyday conversations, we use language in a number of different ways. We speak literally, figuratively, metaphorically, and we use such literary tools as analogy, simile, and hyperbole. We must keep in mind that the biblical writers also are allowed to use all these tools in conveying the story they have to tell. There are places where hyperbole is used to drive home a point, or a metaphor is used to suggest an important nuance. To give an obvious example, to say that Jesus is "the bread of life" is not to say that Jesus is literally a loaf of bread. Rather, the intent is to convey the importance of Jesus to our spiritual health and our life of discipleship.

Further, to accept the Bible as Scripture does not mean that every one of the biblical narratives is to be taken as history in our contemporary sense of simply reporting the facts. So, for example, whether Jesus delivered the Sermon on the Mount with exactly and only the words recorded in Matthew 5–7 matters little. That Matthew 5–7 accurately relates the content of Jesus's teaching matters a great deal. The Gospel writers pick and choose materials from the life of Jesus in order to give us the four Gospels. But to treat the Gospels as Scripture does not require that we view the Gospels as the evening news.

Finally, to accept the Bible as Scripture does not require that we force an artificial unity and consistency over the Scriptures as a whole. God progressively reveals his intentions to us. Readers are told in the Old Testament to observe the rule of "an eye for an eye and a tooth for a tooth," but in Matthew 5, Jesus gives different instructions. Now, we are to love our enemies and pray for those who persecute us. The progressive nature of Scripture is discernible, but it requires us to be attentive. God is going somewhere, and this is evident in the way the biblical narratives are constructed and assembled.

Narrative and Divine Revelation

Throughout the history of the Christian tradition, the church has overwhelmingly held that Scripture communicates God's revelation to us; in some sense, God speaks to us through Scripture. But the church has not adopted one single theory of inspiration, which has allowed for differing interpretations of what exactly it means to affirm that the Bible is "God's Word." Regardless of the particular theory, the fact that the Bible is understood to be divine revelation explains why we rightly respect Scripture and accept, perhaps in somewhat different senses, its authority over us. It is only a small step from our great reverence for Scripture as divine revelation to thinking that each individual verse or passage stands equally as God's Word *even apart* from its contextual setting. We reason that this particular passage is just as much God's revelation as all the rest, and since God's revelation is trustworthy, I need not read all of Scripture to apply this passage. Unfortunately, such reasoning fails to understand the manner in which good narratives are to be read and understood. And to use a method of reading that does not adequately take into account the narrative structure of Scripture is to open the door to a good deal of misunderstanding.

Imagine that you go down to the local bookstore and purchase a novel, say, a good crime drama. You take the book home and settle in for a good evening of reading. Not being a particularly patient reader, you skip ahead to one of the later chapters where you discover that the lead character has become a member of a local mob. Well, right away, you begin to draw conclusions about the nature of the lead character, about his life, about what you think would constitute his just treatment, and so on. However, if you had started at the beginning, you would have found out that this character was not a member of the mob but rather an undercover police agent. Further, if you had read the prologue, the death of the lead character's older brother from a drug over-dose would have given you more insight into how this particular character had developed over the course of the story. In short, by reading the ending first, you would have missed too much and failed to properly understand what is going on. A good story involves character development. Different scenes serve as the opportunities for that development. There are problems and challenges the characters face and have to resolve. And the order and manner in which all these things happen matter. Stories move from beginning to end, unveiling their contents as the story is told. The "jump-to-the-end" way of reading short-circuits the story and leads us into error.

Could our approach to the Bible be understood similarly? A period of at least a thousand years spans the writing of the first biblical books to the writing of the last one. Many of these different books are attributed to different writers from different periods within those thousand years. How, then, is it reasonable to see the Bible as similar to a great novel? Novels are generally written within a relatively short time frame by a single human author. Neither of these things is true of the Bible. And not all of Scripture is narrative in form. There are songs and poetry (such as Psalms and the Song of Songs), wisdom sayings (Proverbs), letters (such as Romans and Titus), as well as historical or quasihistorical narratives (such as Genesis and the Gospels). Are we not stretching things too far to try to think of Scripture along the lines of a single narrative? I do not think so, for a number of reasons.

First, while the biblical writings span many centuries, the fact that the tradition has seen them as God's revelation means that we can consider these writings as the story of God's interaction with humanity. In some sense, then, God is the Bible's author (either of the texts themselves or of the events the texts report).

Second, in telling the story of God's interaction with his people there is room to include different subgenres. For example, the book of Proverbs constitutes the wisdom sayings given to the people at one point in the story, the Psalms are like a community hymnbook, and so on. Some texts are more directly storylike than others, but they all fit together to tell God's story with regard to his creation of and interaction with the world.

Third, since God is driven by a particular goal or set of goals, it is the presence and action of God within the biblical narratives that gives them their unity. This is what holds the biblical writings together as one story—the story about God and his creation. The biblical writings bear similarity to epic stories enough for us to read them in the way we would read a good narrative as we seek to understand what God intends to reveal through Scripture.

Thinking of the Bible as narrative also relates to the role the Bible is to play in forming us as God's people. Why has God given Scripture *to us*? I would argue that the goal of Scripture is not primarily to convey information (though, of course, this is part of its purpose) but rather to identify us as and to form us into the image of Christ. God does not merely want us to *do* this or that; he wants us also to *be* a particular kind of people. The biblical narratives, then, are not given merely to convey rules about what God wants us to do. Rather, they give us stories that identify who we are (we are the people whose story this is) and form us into persons who see things as God sees them and who make the kinds of judgments God would make. As we "live" in the narratives, we begin to live in the world as defined by the Bible (rather than nonbiblical definitions). The perspective of the biblical narratives becomes the basis for our judgments and behavior. Mere instructions or commands alone cannot accomplish this deeper task of formation and transformation.

Children often imitate characters after reading about them in a story or seeing them in a movie. They will dress up like Batman or Wonder Woman in order to "save the world." Adults see movies like *Hotel Rwanda* and find that they can no longer see the world in quite the same way. Powerful narratives impact and change us in powerful ways. Of course, both good and bad formation are possible and do occur. This is why it matters so much which narratives we allow to have a formative effect upon us. Consider how we often relate the events of narratives to our own lives. When my daughter played basketball in high school, I would never respond to the question "Did Sara have a good game last night?" by simply giving the statistics. ("She scored seventeen points on 65 percent shooting from the field and had six assists!") No; I tell a story. "In the first quarter, the game moved pretty slowly. She played good defense, but didn't have many scoring opportunities. Just at the end of the half, she made a driving layup and was fouled. Though in pain, she hit the free throw that gave the team a one-point margin at the half...." We retell our lives in narrative form because narratives are engaging and more effectively convey what happened than a reductionism that simply reports bare facts. For effective, engaging communication and formative interaction, narratives have a unique power—a power that God has fully utilized in conveying to us revelation about himself as he interacts with his creation.

Voices to the contrary notwithstanding, narratives cannot be set aside once a set of abstract principles have been extracted. Reading Scripture in this reductionist way tends to lead us to see Scripture as a rule book, and the formative nature of narrative is generally displaced and lost in the process.

Let us briefly consider the basic components of narratives and the way in which they instruct us in better understanding the biblical narratives. All good narratives have a relatively stable set of components from which the infinite variety of stories is constructed. Perhaps the two most significant parts of all narratives are the set of characters and the plot around which the interactions between the characters unfold. Stories have both protagonists and antagonists. The protagonist is generally the good person and functions as the centerpiece of the story. The antagonist is generally the foil for the protagonist. The conflict between the two generally constitutes the storyline. (Of course, things are not always so simple; many stories seem to blur the lines between good and evil.)

One point that Christians often seem to miss in our contemporary "me-first" culture is that in the Bible, God, not humanity, is the main character. God establishes the overarching theme and direction of Scripture, and God works consistently throughout Scripture to bring that end into reality. Unfortunately, far too much of what passes for preaching and writing in Christian circles today makes the basic error of thinking that humanity is the main character of the Bible. When we get this point backward, our focus in all our reading of Scripture is threatened. We focus on human wrongdoing rather than God's grace; on our need to be restored rather than God's acts of restoration; and on how we benefit from a relationship with God rather than the simple fact that we were created for relationship with God. One way to understand the overarching message of Scripture is to say that God is creating a world of creatures for relationship with himself. All of the story and all of God's acts, then, are focused to bring such a world into being. This does not underestimate the importance of humanity but rather orders things properly.

In the narrative that is the Christian Bible, God is the main character and we are supporting characters. This biblical narrative is about God creating a world and filling it with creatures for relationship with him. Since God has created us for relationship, there is no other basis for our genuine fulfillment apart from relationship with God. All other alternative ways of pursuing fulfillment are illusory. The narrative of Scripture began with God's initial creative act. God's creative activity continues as he seeks to shape us in order to be the relational partners that he intends. There is a plot to the narrative that begins in Genesis, and the details of that plot unfold over time. Just as with any good story, more and more details become available as the story progresses toward its final resolution or climax. As a consequence, it matters where in the story we are and where in the story we are reading. For example, Christians tend to hold that the life of Jesus is the high point of God's revelation in Scripture, and that the ministry of Jesus shines a light backward onto earlier texts, helping us to understand them more fully. Later parts of the story tend to illumine earlier parts. As we read and study Scripture, we cannot lose sight of the importance of relating the various parts of the texts to each other in order to make a proper reading and understanding of those texts more likely.

There are two other aspects of good narratives that are important to our understanding of the biblical narratives. First, it is essential that we have a common set of terms and concepts that enable us to hear what the biblical narratives intend to say to us—a common vocabulary, if you will. One might immediately wonder how this can be, given that the biblical narratives were written in Greek and Hebrew over the course of several centuries. This is one area where the work of biblical scholars is of critical importance. They research the biblical cultures and their use of language in an attempt to translate the biblical stories into contemporary terms and idioms. This work must continue indefinitely given the evolving nature of language. Beyond the various interpretations and translations, though, some basic study in the sociocultural conditions at the time the various parts of the Bible were written will provide additional insight into how the terms and phrases used in the Bible might have been used in that sociocultural setting. Doing this, of course, can only enhance our grasp of Scripture's meaning.

The second thing the reader needs to watch for in studying the Bible is the way that the different writers use each other's ideas to deepen their own points. The technical term for this is *intertextual reference*. In such cases, one writer assumes that a reader is going to be familiar with the writings of another. By using common terms, the second writer appropriates ideas from the previous writer into his own work. For example, when the Gospel writers use the term "Son of Man" to refer to Jesus, they assume that the reader will be aware of how this term is used, say, in the writings of the book of Daniel. When the references between writers are missed, we too often assign a meaning to what we are reading that misses the point or, worse, we assign the meaning to the term or phrase that we would have given it had we used it. Words and phrases evolve over time, and we simply must not assume that what they mean to us now is what they meant in that culture then.

As the plot unfolds in the biblical narrative, writers frequently use these sorts of references as shorthand ways to bring together a variety of texts. Rikki Watts argues that the writer of Mark uses the idea of "exodus" from Isaiah in order to describe what Jesus is doing.[4] Watts points to particular ways in which the writer of Mark "codes" his text so that the reader will know that he intends for them to see in Jesus the new exodus Isaiah foresaw. Other examples include how Matthew borrows the term "virgin" from Isaiah 7, and how Mark cites the same prophet as a recognition of John the Baptist's role to "prepare the way of the Lord." We have already considered the use of the term "Son of Man," and it is doubtful that we can rightly understand its use in the Gospels without spending some time in the book of Daniel. Without that engagement, we tend to think we already know what the terms mean based on the common meanings that occur within our own subtraditions.

The Scriptures are filled with cross-references that we overlook every day because we simply have not been trained to look for them. Let me be clear: I am not suggesting that the Bible cannot be understood apart from mastering these techniques. What I am suggesting is that attention to these issues opens us to the richness of the biblical narratives and helps us to understand them more deeply than we would otherwise. The basic call of the gospel to restored relationship with God is fairly straightforward. However, the issue we are considering—the shape of public life and political institutions in relation to God's expectations—is much more complex. These are not surface matters, and we shouldn't be surprised that a more involved method of study of those narratives is required.

Reading Scripture: Conclusions

In this chapter, we have considered ways of becoming better readers of the Bible and thus of becoming better at understanding God's expectations for us. In the first part of the chapter, we examined several popular prooftexts regarding the relationship between Christian faith and public policies and institutions. We found each to be less than helpful. Next, we outlined four guidelines for reading Scripture. These included:

1. Avoiding prooftexting by more aggressively mining Scripture for materials that deal with the questions and issues we are facing.

2. Recognizing the importance of immediate and broader contexts for developing a more thorough understanding of how different terms and phrases are being used.

3. Resisting moving directly from texts to contemporary application and instead taking time to try to understand the underlying motivation for many of the things God commands or expects.

4. Learning to read the entire Bible holistically so that we gain an increasingly firmer grasp on what Scripture is all about.

In the final section, we argued that a narrative understanding of Scripture brings together these guidelines with other issues around the concept of intertextual reference in order to enable us to best grasp the content of the biblical narratives.

All of this, of course, suggests that reading Scripture is a bit more complicated than we are often led to believe. Yet observing even the simple set of ideas we have discussed in this chapter will go a long way in helping us to become better readers of Scripture. Of course, even strict adherence to these guidelines for reading and applying Scripture will not guarantee error-free interpretation nor will it assure that all our discussion partners will agree with us. It will, however, give us a better place from which to understand Scripture and to see how God's intentions relate to the place of both private and public institutions in realizing the kind of communities that he desires for us.

3

The God of Abraham, Isaac, Jacob, and Jesus

The concept of God I inherited led me to believe that God was out to get me. By now, I have heard enough to know that this was hardly a sentiment unique to me. All the preachers I heard would have affirmed, at least theoretically, the biblical claim that "God is love." Nevertheless, there was a remarkably consistent undertone (and, frankly, too often an overtone) of judgment and condemnation present in virtually every sermon. God was consistently painted as the difficult taskmaster who was impossible to please—so impossible, in fact, that God had to become human in order to make up for our shortcomings. We were frequently reminded that the vast majority of things we did were surely things God hated. There is, of course, a very important element of truth to a view that properly recognizes human sin. However, did it really help to paint God not just as angry all the time but as *angry at me* all the time?

In churches where the wrath of God was emphasized, the passages most frequently cited in sermons were those that focused on human sinfulness as compared to God's holiness. For example, many sermons reminded us that "the wages of sin are death" and that "there is none righteous, no not one." All of our goodness combined was the equivalent of "filthy rags" in God's sight. Hearing these pictures of the hopeless state of humanity, we were reminded that the holiness of God is so pure that no sinful human could survive God's presence.

It never quite seemed to occur to these folks that we need not disparage humanity in order to exalt God. In other words, we can accept human sinfulness and God's affirmation of and love for his creation while also realizing that God's holiness does not depend on emphasizing human perversity. If God's holiness seems great compared to human sinfulness, imagine how great it would appear if compared to the best of human behavior! Yet it seems that we too often become prey to Nietzsche's claim that for God to be everything, humanity had to become nothing.[1] This tendency toward human negation, while useful for the short-term goal of encouraging conversion, ultimately turned many away. It need not have.

What sort of image of God did you inherit? There is a particularly powerful film by Curt Cloninger entitled *God Views*.[2] In it Cloninger explores several different yet popular ways of conceiving of God. The very first one characterizes God as the "Cosmic Sheriff." God rides around the world on a horse named Guilt looking for any who may have broken one or more of his many laws. When he finds a trespasser, he gleefully uses his cosmic six-shooter to deliver the appropriate punishment for the infraction. This God forgives grudgingly because it is part of the deal, not because it is central to his nature to be forgiving. This God hardly does justice to the biblical view of God. Unfortunately, this was the view of God to which many of us were exposed during our formative years. We saw God as sitting somewhere "up there," attentive to our every move, primarily looking for an excuse to zap us for an indiscretion—and no indiscretion was perceived as too small. Martin Luther must have had a similar view of God when he admitted that he feared and hated God more than he loved him.[3]

Unfortunately, I suspect too many can imagine a human father who might (or perhaps did) treat his children in such a critical and judgmental fashion. How could one expect those exposed to such an unhealthy parental model to develop healthy images of self and God? Would this not hinder their ability to trust and engage in healthy relationships? When one perceives the most important people in their lives as being unforgiving and impossible to please, one develops a strongly critical spirit and rarely has a positive sense of self-worth. At one point in his film, Cloninger observes that little is more influential in how we live our everyday lives than our conception of God. We live, in other words, in accordance with how we conceive of God—whether that is of God as nonexistent, the loving Father portrayed in Scripture, an autocratic dictator, or the impossible-to-please parent.

Of course, not everyone grew up thinking about God as the Cosmic Sheriff, and Cloninger's film is delightful in capturing the popular alternatives. There is "God the Butler": the God to whom we pray only when we are in trouble or want something. Accordingly, we conceive of God as existing to serve us rather than the other way around. The relationship is one based on utility—God is a useful tool for us when it comes to living the life we desire. We pray to God when we want something, expecting him to attend to our needs.

Next, there is "God the Cosmic Mechanic." In this view, God's primary role is to keep the universe running smoothly, or at least as smoothly as possible. God does not have time to worry about damaged relationships, hurt feelings, or things like vocational discernment. God is just too busy managing the universe to be bothered by the minutiae of our daily lives. Better to leave him alone in his task of keeping the universe from falling into disrepair than to bother him with things like our own health or happiness. This, in a sense, is the opposite of God the Butler.

Then, Cloninger gives us "God the Old Timer." Here, God is the old man with the gray beard. He used to be very involved in the lives of his creatures, but now he is old and withdrawn. According to this view, God has wound the universe up like a clock and is now simply watching things unwind, constantly amazed at the creativity of humans. He neither wants much from humans nor offers much. He has tea with the angels every hundred years or so but otherwise reclines in his rocker on the porch. Senility is rapidly approaching.

Another popular view of God Cloninger calls "God in a box." church people have put constraints on what God can do and where he can go. Mostly, they keep him in the box to show off to others. "Here's our God—ain't he cute?" they ask. But they don't let God out of the box for fear he might scare potential church members. The big and bold God—the one who created the universe—is simply too powerful and frightening for the genteel folks of the twenty-first century. This view of God allows us to maintain the illusion of being more in control than we are.

Of course, all of these views are inadequate as conceptions of the God of Abraham, Isaac, and Jacob, the God presented in Scripture. Yet they are views that many of us hold, and therein lies the problem: to the extent that we miss God's nature, we will almost certainly err in understanding what he expects of us. No matter how much we might want to live in ways that conform to God's intentions for us, a seriously flawed grasp of who God is will prevent us from properly grasping those intentions and expectations. One cannot live in conformity to what one does not understand. This is why we must first inquire into the nature of God and consider how a proper understanding of God's nature informs the questions we are undertaking in this book. What insights about the structure of our public life might we gain from a better understanding of the God whom we are enjoined to imitate?

The characteristics we develop in imitation of God influence how we engage with others at every level of social interaction. Because political life, properly understood, involves how we organize and order ourselves into societies, it follows that our character development has a profound impact on the nature of our common public life. To know and imitate God will necessarily impact the manner in which we understand and live out that common public life.

Our understanding of God influences us in other ways also. In the first volume of his *Systematic Theology*, theologian Paul Tillich uses the idea of "ultimate concern" to describe the manner in which the idea of God pervades our thinking.[4] In essence, he says that whatever our ultimate concern is, that which is most important to us, functions as "god" for us. Of course, he is not suggesting that everyone's ultimate concern is really "god" in some metaphysical sense but rather that this ultimate concern is the thing that most captures our attention and imagination. It becomes that which we order our lives around. Atheists who explicitly deny the existence of God or agnostics who confess they have no idea whether God exists still have things in their lives that function as their own ultimate concerns. This could be some value, such as the classical humanist notion of the intrinsic value of humanity, a commitment to the equal treatment of all so that all might flourish. Or perhaps it is a commitment to scientific rationalism, the belief that the sciences hold the answer to human well-being. Or perhaps it is as mundane as the goal to become the best golfer possible.

This ultimate concern, whatever it is, is the thing that serves as the ordering principle in our lives. If we are Christians then the God of our Lord Jesus Christ should be the thing around which we organize and order our lives. To recall Cloninger's comment, the way in which we conceive of God (or god) is the most important factor in determining how we live and interact with others. To be more specifically political, if we think God is apolitical, we might tend to a sectarian withdrawal from the political aspects of life. If we think God is mostly concerned with matters of private piety, then we will understand the intersections of faith and politics in one way. If we think God is most concerned that we structure society in ways to protect "the least of these," then we will understand the intersections of faith and politics in quite another way. And if we think God is concerned about both, there will be yet another way of thinking about these things. For the remainder of this chapter, we will focus our attention first on aspects of God's nature and then on the implications the divine nature should have for how we order our common public lives.

Father, Son, and Holy Spirit: The Trinitarian God

The early church found itself in quite a theological quandary. On the one hand, as heirs to the Hebrew Scriptures and the basic outline of the Jewish faith, Christians had to affirm the *shema*—the claim from Deuteronomy 6:4 that the God of Abraham, Isaac, and Jacob is not a polytheistic group of deities but rather one

God. On the other hand, from early on Christians prayed to and worshiped both Jesus and the Spirit. The resolution, completed with the work of the Cappadocian fathers, was to affirm that God is both three and one: God is one with respect to his nature, but this one divine nature is expressed in a divine community of the three persons of Father, Son, and Holy Spirit.[5]

Another influential voice in the history of the church, Richard of St. Victor, reflects on the fact that the communal life of God takes expression in three persons. Why not only two? Why not more? Richard argued that three is the number of persons necessary to embody perfect love. If there are only two persons, then the love the two have for each other could be selfish. With three persons involved, however, each person must love both of the others as well as desire that the other two perfectly love each other. Perhaps the human family is the closest analogy to the inner life of God: parents love each other and love their child but also desire loving relationships between each of the other two as well.

The emphasis on the communal nature of the Trinity has come to be called "social trinitarianism." This position makes explicit the idea that the three persons of the Trinity make up a society composed of three persons living in relationships of perfect love. Of course, the three persons of the Trinity make up a more perfect society than can ever be realized among humans. Each member of the Trinity interacts with the others in a love so perfect that the early church invoked the image of a dance to describe the complete harmony of the Father, Son, and Spirit. Nothing about them is not fully shared in mutual love.

What would it be like to imitate a God whose inner life can be characterized by such harmony? This has profound implications for a shared public life. If the God we are to imitate can only be properly characterized as a society, what implications does that have for our societies?

Though we cannot explore the doctrine of the Trinity in depth, it is worth thinking about the broad implications of the doctrine for understanding what it means to be created in God's image. If we are created in the image of a God who is a society of persons in relationship, then we cannot escape the conclusion that we humans have been created as relational beings. We are destined for relationships, first with God and then with our fellow human beings. Just as the persons of the Trinity live in mutual, self-giving love, so we are created to engage the others around us in this way. We are to live in relationships of mutual interdependence.

Yet we live in a culture rooted in rugged individualism. We are constantly encouraged to pull ourselves up by our own bootstraps, to look out for "number one," and to exalt personal responsibility. The popular vision of human autonomy argues that our goal is to avoid dependence on others and instead to become self-sufficient and independent. Neither of these positions, dependence or autonomous independence, can do justice to the call to be imitators of the trinitarian God. Of course, we are not to live in slavish dependence upon others so that we are always takers but never givers. Nor are we to live in such independence that we tend only to ourselves and never to our neighbors. Again, to imitate the triune nature of God in our interactions with others is to realize that we are enjoined to live in communities of *mutual interdependence* characterized by the self-giving love embodied and expressed in the life of God. This is as simple as the command to "love your neighbor as yourself." Yet the development of genuine and mutual interdependence is both complex and difficult; it runs counter to our normal self-centeredness.

God Is Love

The term that perhaps best captures God's interaction with humans throughout the biblical narratives is "love." We are told that

God's love extends to all his creation and we are given an image of God as one whose every action is guided first and foremost by his unfailing love. Perhaps one of the most interesting passages of Scripture is 1 John 4:8, which states that "God *is* love." The claim is not that God *has* love or that God is *loving*; rather the author is starkly identifying God with the concept of love itself. Now, I do not want to try to hang too much on one verse, but when coupled with the consistent theme of God's love throughout Scripture, it seems we are invited to conclude that love is not just one attribute among many. Instead, we must see love as being so central to God's nature that we can affirm that his every action is guided by it. What would it mean to take seriously the call to imitate a God who is characterized preeminently by love? How would imitating such a God lead us to interact with each other in our common public lives?

If God's love extends to all his creation, then we have to think seriously about what it means to have been entrusted to be stewards of God's creation, for example. The affirmation from Genesis 1 indicating that humans are given "dominion" over the earth must be seen as conveying the idea of having been entrusted with the stewardship of the earth. We may not simply exploit the earth for our own gain; rather we are to tend to it, care for it, and remember that future generations will benefit or suffer based upon how well we exercise that stewardship.

"Love" is a term used so frequently today that we should wonder if we really understand what it means to say that we love someone. Too often we use the word to mean little more than that we have warm, fuzzy feelings for someone. While I suspect the biblical notion of love does not exclude such feelings, to leave it there would be inadequate. To love someone is to desire their long-term well-being and to be willing to engage in acts of self-sacrifice to bring it about. John expresses this idea when he says, "No one has greater love than this, to lay down one's life for one's friends" (John 15:13). Or, regarding the love the Father exhibited in the sending of the Son, the apostle Paul tells us that while we were yet hostile to God, he sent his Son (Rom. 5:8). Of course, the injunction for us to love our neighbors as ourselves makes very explicit the degree to which our love of others is to extend. Have you ever thought about what it would mean for us genuinely to love our neighbors as we love ourselves? When we are hungry, we feed ourselves; when we are cold, we warm ourselves; when we are thirsty, we drink; and when we are guilty of wrongdoing, we forgive ourselves. If we loved our neighbors as ourselves, would we not do as much for them?

All of this invites the question, Who is the neighbor we are to love as we love ourselves? Jesus answers this question in the parable of the Good Samaritan. The answer was, no doubt, shocking to those listening to Jesus. Since the person who demonstrates neighborly love in this parable is a despised Samaritan, Jesus says that we are to be a neighbor even to those we are most inclined to dislike. That all are to be considered neighbors to be "loved as we love ourselves" is amplified when, at the end of the Sermon on the Mount, we are enjoined to imitate the perfection of God (Matt. 5:48). How is the goodness and love of God demonstrated? By the fact that God blesses without regard to merit, causing the sun to shine and the rain to fall on the just and unjust alike. In the same part of the Sermon on the Mount, Jesus contrasts the "old command" to love our neighbors with the "new command" to love even our enemies. How easily we constrain our lives—and even more, our deployment of resources—to "our own."

As we put these pieces together, we begin to get a picture that is remarkably challenging. Most of us accept the responsibility to love our immediate circle of families and friends. Yet this alone is not adequate for those who would imitate the love of God. We must love all of our neighbors, even the ones we are inclined least to like—even our enemies. To imitate a God who loves to such a great degree is by no means an easy thing. Yet to aim for anything less is to miss one of the central calls of Scripture. As we work our way through these issues, we will bolster this call to love of neighbor and, in due course, relate it to Christian views of public policies and institutions.

God as Human: The Incarnation

For Christians, the life of Jesus changes everything. New Testament scholar N. T. Wright refers to the life of Jesus as the culmination of the story of salvation—God's great rescue mission to reconcile humans to himself.[6] Christians have used the term "incarnation" to describe the event whereby one of the persons of the Trinity steps into human history and takes on human form, entering fully into the human condition. Our concern is with how the incarnation helps us develop a more complete picture of God's nature.

Christians have argued that there are three reasons for the incarnation, and each of them is relevant to our understanding of God's nature. First, the sending of the Son serves God's intention to heal the broken relationship between himself and his human creatures. While groups throughout the history of the church have had different ideas about the details of how this was accomplished, there is broad agreement that Jesus's ministry, death, and resurrection make possible the restoration God intended. We need not debate those details here but rather simply recognize that God's loving nature is concretely expressed in his willingness to be the initiator of restoration. When God saw the world in need of his presence, he acted decisively.

In addition, Jesus's ministry of healing and teaching concretely demonstrates to humanity the self-giving love of God's inner life. God's loving nature comes to expression in the world in his initiative to reach out to those in need. The death of Jesus on the cross is the definitive expression of God's love—no price is too great to free the captives, heal the sick, and restore relationship. We would do well to pause and ponder the implications of following and imitating One whose sacrifice shows no limits—and what it would mean to live out such love in the world.

Second, the incarnation shows us what God is like. The incarnation is the ultimate object lesson regarding God's nature. In Jesus we see what God is like, and we see those aspects of the divine nature that we as humans are to imitate. Jesus gives a revelation of God's nature that is intelligible to us. Jesus's life and ministry are the primary places to gather information about God.

Third, Jesus reveals to us how humanity, as God intended it, is to be and act. In Jesus, we finally see what God has always intended for all of us. Jesus is the culmination of God's creation of humanity, the ultimate moral exemplar for humans. It is easy to imagine why Paul would use the language of "second Adam" to describe Jesus (1 Cor. 15:22). Numerous other passages make the case. Some show that Jesus succeeded where Adam and Eve failed, others that Jesus avoided temptations to which God's people continually fall prey. To be an imitator of Jesus is to live in accordance with God's expectations. In due course we will take up the question of what implications follow from the imitation of Christ for public life.

Many passages from the New Testament make clear that imitation of Jesus is very intimately connected with taking up our cross and following the Crucified One. The self-giving way of living that puts the interests of others first is at the root of the trinitarian nature of the God who is characterized as love. What more powerful way of demonstrating this than to lay down our life for a friend? One can see why it has often been said that the incarnation turns our normal way of thinking about life, community, and power completely upside down.

God's Holiness

"I, the Lord your God, am holy." One need not look very hard within the biblical texts to find this affirmation. For example, in Leviticus 19:2, God tells Moses to say to the people, "You shall be holy, for I the LORD your God am holy." Here, God's holiness is coupled very closely with certain expectations that God has for his hearers. Specifically, God does not merely affirm his own holiness but also states explicitly his intention that humans be imitators of his holiness. This makes our interest in determining what it means to be holy all the more pressing, and the subsequent content of Leviticus 19 begins to flesh out what God intends. It is interesting that the characteristics of holiness laid out here can be summarized by what Jesus called the two great commandments: love the Lord your God with all your heart, mind, soul, and strength, and love your neighbor as yourself. Consider just a few examples from Leviticus 19:

- Honor your parents
- Keep the Lord's sabbaths
- Do not worship anything other than the Lord your God
- During harvest time, for grain or grapes, leave some for the poor and sojourners
- Treat others with integrity (do not lie, cheat, or steal)
- Welcome the strangers in your land
- Make fair and impartial judgments

- Do not take advantage of others
- Love your neighbor as yourself
- Remember to give to God appropriate praise and sacrifice

Between each of these sets of commands is the statement "For I am the Lord your God," as if to remind the reader at every turn that the commands themselves are rooted in the very nature of the God who is characterized first and foremost in this passage as the Holy One. To live the life that pleases God—that is, to be holy—is to live out these commands and others like them.

If we move forward to the New Testament, at the end of the first section of the Sermon on the Mount we find Jesus issuing the following injunction to his hearers: "You, therefore, must be perfect, as your heavenly Father is perfect." Once again, we see the call for us to be imitators of God—that is, what God intends for humans to be is rooted in and demonstrated by his own nature. The term Jesus used here is a form of the Greek word *telos*, which connotes such ideas as end or purpose or completion, and as noted in the translation cited here, the idea of perfection. While the underlying Greek word for "perfection" is not the Greek term usually translated "holy" or "holiness," the surrounding context of Matthew 5 carries with it the sense of moral or ethical purity that is rooted in the divine nature. Jesus's call in the Sermon is a New Testament form of the call of Leviticus for humans to be holy.

If we examine the entirety of Matthew 5, we will find that the call to be perfect can be reduced to the two great commandments, just as we saw in Leviticus 19. In short, the life that pleases God, that lives out faithfully the holiness to which we are called, is a life that orients itself properly to our Creator (i.e., we love God with all our heart, mind, soul, and strength) and to "the other" (i.e., we are to love our neighbors as ourselves). However, in the immediate context of Matthew 5:48 (vv. 43–48), we find that the divine perfection is directly connected with loving and blessing others *without regard to merit*. In fact, this love without regard to merit goes so far as to require us to love our enemies and pray for our persecutors. The extent to which this is rooted in the imitation of God is obvious: while we were yet hostile to God, he sent his Son; while the soldiers persecute Jesus on the cross, he prays for their forgiveness; and the very act of incarnation itself is an act whereby the Son reaches beyond the divine life to offer himself to and for his human creatures. To be holy—that is, to live the life that pleases God—is to orient ourselves beyond ourselves in order to love God and others with utter abandon.

If we think about holiness along these lines, then holiness is first and foremost a *relational* concept. The term "holy" is rarely used in Christian circles. When it is used, it is often limited to two applications. First, the term is used when we speak of the Holy Spirit, the third person of the Trinity. Or perhaps some of us think of it in terms of the Holy Bible. In these cases, though, I wonder if we simply use the term without much thought, as just part of a title. Second, some strands of the Christian tradition use the term in a more negative sense. We are to be holy, but being holy is defined largely in terms of things that we *do not* do, that is, in terms of certain sins to be avoided. However, the first thing we should think of with respect to the term "holy" is a certain way of being in relation. Go back again to the list of behaviors in Leviticus 19 and note the connection with rightly loving God and neighbor. Holiness is about imitating the relational nature of the triune God and, as such, is crucial for understanding God's nature.

God and Oppression

Few things displease God more than when his children are victims of oppression and exploitation. The paradigmatic expression of this comes in the story of the exodus. In fact, exodus-like events appear in different forms throughout Scripture, and some scholars take it to be the central event of the Bible. The story begins in Genesis when Joseph, the son of Jacob, is sold as a slave but ends up as a top advisor to the pharaoh in Egypt. The rest of the family, including Jacob, move to Egypt as a consequence of an extended famine.

Because Joseph advised the pharaoh shrewdly, Egypt had plenty of food and was able to absorb the migrating Israelites. The family did well in their new home until a pharaoh came to power. In other words, a few generations later, the favored position of the Israelites was lost, and the new pharaoh saw the Israelites as cheap labor to exploit. They were enslaved and put to work on various projects. At the beginning of the book of Exodus, the Israelites bewail their condition, crying out to God for deliverance. God hears their cry and begins a series of interventions that ultimately lead to freedom for the Israelites. The liberation of the Israelites via the various acts God accomplishes through Moses becomes the series of events that identifies the Israelite people—they are the ones to whom God brought freedom by both outsmarting and overpowering the ruler of Egypt.

The exodus story helps us to see God's nature and concerns as he interacts with oppression. First, we should note that there was nothing illegal about slavery at that time. God's concern for the right treatment of others extends beyond what is simply legal according to the laws of humanity. Rather, God is concerned for those on the margins, those who are weak, or those who are in some way vulnerable. God did not call the Israelites to be his people because they were a strong people, but rather because they were weak. God is most concerned for those we would consider "underdogs." God eventually used his power to bring about a new reality for the Israelites.

If we move forward in time to when God provides directions regarding the shape of political and economic life, we see some very interesting commandments. From an economic perspective, God explicitly commands things like the Years of Jubilee, the Years of Release, and some very odd (by twenty-first-century standards) collateral laws. God instructs his people to welcome the strangers who come to their lands. As he gives these instructions, God reminds them that they were once strangers themselves. We will examine these references more in the next chapter. Here we merely note how God not only ends the oppression of the Israelites but also gives them instructions to prevent them from exploiting others in the future.

By the time we come to Isaiah, the themes of the exodus are picked up again in order to speak of a different kind of liberation—humanity's liberation from sin. We would be mistaken to see this as a replacement for God's concern for liberation from physical oppression. Rather, we should see it as an expansion into both the personal and the public spheres. In fact, there is a very close connection between freedom from our "private" sins and freedom from the institutional sins that create exploitative and oppressive public institutions.

Finally, we would be remiss not to note the strong expression of themes of liberation and release from oppression that appear in Jesus's mission statement of Luke 4. In verses 16–19, we read the following:

> When he came to Nazareth, where he had been brought up, he went to the synagogue on the sabbath day, as was his custom. He stood up to read, and the scroll of the prophet Isaiah was given to him. He unrolled the scroll and found the place where it was written: "The Spirit of the Lord is upon me, because he has anointed me to bring good news to the poor. He has sent me to proclaim release to the captives and recovery of sight to

the blind, to let the oppressed go free, to proclaim the year of
the Lord's favor."

Several physical ailments are explicitly named. This is no list
of overly-spiritualized problems but rather very concrete ailments that humans face. Particularly, God expresses concern for
the poor, marginalized, lame, blind, and deaf. Those who are left
behind by the normal priorities of the world are a priority to
God. Oppression and exploitation cannot be reduced merely to
freedom from personal or private sin. Rather, God is concerned
to free humans from every kind of sin, private and institutional,
that prevents human flourishing. This is the mission of God as
expressed through Jesus. This is what Jesus's ministry is all about.

God's Patience

Sometimes discussions about God's nature skip over the idea of
patience altogether, but it is far too important to our objective to
omit it here. While many passages talk about God's patience or
forbearance, I want to focus on the *goals* of God's patience. In other
words, rather than simply talking about what it means for God
to be patient, I am more interested in *why* God is patient. God's
patience is closely related to his love for his creatures. For example,
sometimes people are patient because they are unsure of what to
do or because of their inability to deal with the challenges they
face. This absence of action can be interpreted as patience. God,
however, is never impotent in the face of challenges nor is he ever
at a loss for what to do. God patiently gives people opportunities
to respond to his grace. This idea is given paradigmatic expression
in a passage from 2 Peter: "The Lord . . . is patient with you, not
wanting any to perish, but all to come to repentance" (3:9). God
loves and wants to be in relationship with all people.

As we noted in the previous chapter, an important point in understanding the scriptural narratives is to realize their unfolding, or progressive, nature. How might this be connected with God's patience? God fully realizes that it will take time to move his children to the place where his expectations can be worked out in their lives. At different points in the biblical narratives, God conveys certain expectations. At any given time, these were consistent with where his people were. This is clear in Jesus's intensification of God's law in the Sermon on the Mount. Consider, for example, the Old Testament idea that we are to repay "an eye for an eye and a tooth for a tooth." Compare this to Jesus's instruction in the Sermon:

> You have heard that it was said, "Eye for eye, and tooth for tooth." But I tell you, Do not resist an evil person. If someone strikes you on the right cheek, turn to him the other also. (Matt. 5:38–39 NIV)

When addressing the question of why these things change, Jesus indicates that it was due to our hardness of heart that God accepted something less than his ultimate expectations for us in the past. God was willing to move us toward his ideals over time. As God revealed himself more clearly, however, his expectations for us increased. With the incarnation we have the premier revelation of God, and God's expectations are elevated along with it. God's love and patience led him to move toward his expectations over time—never taking longer than necessary, but also never leaving us unchallenged to move toward them. We must always keep this in mind when appropriating instructions from early in the biblical narratives.

Implications

We began this chapter by arguing that it is important to develop an understanding of God's nature if we are to rightly discern

God's expectations for the manner in which our common life should be structured. It is now time to explore how our findings might provide both a basis and a context for our understanding of public policies and institutions. At this point, we are not ready to consider specific policy proposals or specific governmental forms. (That will come in chapter 6.) We are prepared, however, to draw some general conclusions from our study so far. I use the remainder of this chapter to outline eight potential guidelines.

1. *Because of the biblical injunction to be imitators of God, the discernment of God's expectations for our common lives cannot be separated from discernment of God's nature.* This has been the central thesis of this chapter. The idea, quite simply, is that God has intentions for the way in which our common lives are to be structured. Further, God has created us with those intentions in mind so that his intentions are within our reach. Finally, those intentions align with our having been created in God's image. Recognizing the implications of having been created in God's image and being called to be imitators of God, we see how understanding God's nature is essential to our living in accord with God's intentions for us, both privately and publicly.

2. *God's intentions always aim toward long-term flourishing for all humans.* As our Creator, the way God intends us to structure our common lives will lead to the best environment for human flourishing for the most people. Now, we need not interpret this in a simplistic fashion that precludes hard work or sacrifice. As we all know, sometimes long-term flourishing requires short-term sacrifice. To affirm that God intends for all to flourish does not require public policies or institutions that sugarcoat human existence. The test of public institutions and policies that conform to God's intentions is not that they preclude human suffering, but rather that they eliminate or minimize human suffering

that is not reasonably connected with long-term flourishing. Further, because God intends human flourishing for all, proper imitation of God's nature will lead to flourishing for all—Christian and non-Christian, religious and nonreligious. We would expect nothing less of the God who "sends his rain on the just and the unjust," and he expects no less of us as we interact with those around us.

3. *To live into God's intentions for public life, priority must be given to persons on the margins of society, whatever form that takes.* Many theologians have used the phrase "a preferential option for the poor" to capture the idea that God sides with and favors those in need. To affirm a preferential option for the poor does not mean that the well-to-do are not intended by God to flourish but rather that their flourishing should not come at the cost of those less fortunate. The opportunity to exploit those on the margins of society is always a temptation in economies where businesses aim to maximize profits with little or no restraint. It is too easy for those doing harm to keep those on the margins out of sight and out of mind. Public policies and institutions ought to be structured to prevent this kind of exploitation and to make putting those on the margins "out of sight" much harder. The test of any society, when compared to God's intentions, rests largely on determining how well the "least of these" are doing. Looking ahead, this guideline will undoubtedly have an impact on the free markets we participate in, the business regulations we support, and the tax policies we propose.

4. *Public policies and institutions should be structured so as to encourage, reward, and embody self-giving love.* Our natural tendency is to "look out for number one," or to be most attentive to those closest to us. However, in numerous ways throughout the biblical narratives, God demonstrates a self-giving and loving nature. We have observed that this is best exemplified in the

sending of the Son into the world. The life of Jesus is characterized by a willingness to put others first, and he considered no
sacrifice too great to demonstrate the love of God to us. While
there are complexities involved in putting this into practice with
regard to public policies and institutions, we still fall short of
God's intentions if we have not considered what it would mean
to embody this in every aspect of our lives. At a minimum, we
must be as interested in the flourishing of others as we are in
our own flourishing—ideally, more so. This of course stands
in sharp contrast to our normal tendency to think of our own
personal or national interests ahead of the interests of others.
If this sounds odd or impossible to live up to, that indicates
the extent to which we are misaligned with God's intentions
for us. Our very inability to wrap our mind around this way of
living is evidence of how badly we need social structures that
empower it.

5. *The life of the Trinity demonstrates for us neither independence
nor dependence, but rather mutual interdependence as a way of being.
This mutual interdependency is what God intends for us to model
toward each other.* We have all heard public programs aimed at
serving the poor (and those otherwise on the margins of our
society) criticized for "creating dependency." It is tempting to
wonder just how often this claim is made more out of self-
interest than concern. What greater tool for our own selfishness than an argument that helping those in need is actually a
disservice? There may be situations in which the concern about
creating dependency might be valid. However, to use this as an
excuse to do nothing too easily allows us to avoid one of the
pressing calls of the gospel, namely, to love our neighbors as
we love ourselves.

Similarly, there may be cases where "tough love" is part of a
serious expression of loving others. However, once again, too often

this is used as a rationale for inaction. To assume that all or even many who live on the margins of society do so by personal choice is quite simply mistaken. In the end, offering to do too much for our neighbors is preferable to doing too little. The biblical model, derived from our having been created for relationships where we love others as we love ourselves, is neither dependence nor independence but rather *mutual interdependence*. Whatever forms our public policies and institutions take, they should both realize and encourage this.

6. *We are to live in peace with each other, a peace that is characterized by love of others—even our enemies.* It is significant that Jesus is referenced in Scripture as the Prince of Peace. In fact, it is both central to his identity and his mission to be one who brings and restores peaceful relationships. The peace to which we are called, however, is not the peace of mutual noninterference. God does not call us into relationships where we simply leave each other alone. The peace we are to embody is rooted in the biblical call to love our neighbors and to actively engage them. This is, of course, a much more challenging form of peace—relationships are messy and complex, and they often involve conflict. And it is precisely in our messy and complex relationships of mutual interdependence that we are to embody peace. This requires not only the presence of healthy, nonviolent ways of resolving conflict but also a healthy way of thinking about conflict in the first place: it is not evil in itself but rather the natural outworking of love as we seek to live together in peace. Whatever public policies and institutions we put in place, they must be robust enough to both recognize that conflicts will arise and provide for peaceful conflict resolution.

7. *Public policies and institutions must be carefully constructed to serve human flourishing for all and to minimize the chance of exploitation.* The forms of common life we put into place must not

slant the playing field either for the well-to-do or for the poor. Of course, because of the potential the well-to-do have for exploiting the poor, special care for those on the margins is necessary. At the same time, Scripture is clear that public policies and institutions are not to be set up that allow the poor to exploit the well-to-do either. Both possibilities must be accounted for.

8. *Public policies and institutions must be so constructed as to remind all of us of the great responsibilities that attend wealth.* The story of the rich man and Lazarus in Luke 16 makes it clear that God's expectations for those who have much is that they will use their wealth to benefit others. As we noted earlier, the difficulties the rich man finds himself in by the end of the story do not arise because he did something evil to Lazarus. Rather, they arise simply because he had the resources to help and did not. This should be a frightful passage for most of us who are American, for we are the possessors of great wealth and thus of great obligation. As we shape the institutions and policies that guide our common life, we must keep ever before us the obligation to use our possessions and even our very selves for the benefit of others.

Jesus condemns those who are in the presence of needs but turn a blind eye. Too easily we see what we own coming as a consequence of our own cleverness and hard work. However, all these things come to us without any regard to merit. If the very tools that allow us to flourish are gifts from God, we have an obligation to steward those gifts in a way that serves the kingdom.

These eight guidelines are just that—a set of guidelines that we must keep in mind as we think about, plan, and form our public policies and institutions. They are not by any means specific policy proposals. Nor are they guidelines to be converted directly into policies. Instead, these are the values and commitments that public policies and institutions that conform to God's expectations should embody. They are not exhaustive. I offer them not as finished products but discussion starters. Let us begin a public dialogue that takes these obligations and commitments seriously, and, in so doing, let us form a common life that meets the expectations God had in mind when he created us.

4

Biblical Vignettes

I don't recall the first sporting event at which I saw the sign that simply reads "John 3:16." For a good period of time, that particular sign became quite popular at public events, particularly events that were televised. Undoubtedly, John 3:16 is the single most well-known verse in all of Scripture. This is what makes it possible to simply write "John 3:16" without including any of the verse's content and still effectively communicate that content. Some claim that the entirety of the biblical story is summed up in these few words. In the NRSV, John 3:16 reads, "For God so loved the world that he gave his only Son, so that everyone who believes in him may not perish but may have eternal life."

The focus here is on God's love and the sacrifice he undertook in order to express and embody that love. Further, the verse captures God's intention that his expression of love in Christ should result in the restoration of right relationship with God. But there are concerns with how this passage has been used.

The tradition in which I was raised made the basic message of this verse central to almost every sermon regardless of the biblical passage of the day. While I had a good grasp of the biblical story from the perspective of this one verse, I hardly had a grasp on the biblical story *as a whole*. If I had been pushed to explain in some detail what this verse meant in the broader biblical context, I would have had relatively little to say. What does it mean to "believe in him"? What is the nature of the "perishing" from which one is being saved? And what does it mean to affirm that God "sent his only Son"? Without the broader context of Scripture, it was hard to know how I was supposed to change as a consequence of "believing in him." Were the changes primarily internal or external? Did they relate to my own personal piety, to my life in community, or both? And what would it look like to live that out on a daily basis? Which, of course, brings us back to our central question: how does God intend for us to live together?

Any sermon derived from Scripture has the potential to be used by God to effect change in our lives. However, just as our diets must contain a wide variety of different kinds of food, so also must the biblical diet we feed upon draw from the whole Bible. While spinach is a healthy food, we can't eat spinach and nothing else. Likewise, while John 3:16 is an important biblical text, our ability to live faithfully according to God's expectations for us depends on drawing from all the biblical narratives. We need to be familiar with passages that challenge us to lives of personal piety and devotion but we must also recognize the obligations that our faith places upon us within broader, communal settings. We need both affirmations of behaviors we are to cultivate as well as warnings about those we are to avoid. To achieve this, we need to be formed by the Bible as a whole.

By the way, I do not object to the posting of signs at sporting events or other public events that reference particular Bible verses.

Whether they serve their intended purpose is debatable, but there is no particular reason to object to it. However, we need to make sure that we are being faithful to the entire Bible and not just to our pastor's, or our own, favorite sections. I would venture to say that in an average evangelical church on an average Sunday, the odds would be about three in four that the sermon would come from the New Testament. If we were to take a look at those three in four sermons that come from the New Testament, how many do you suppose come from the Gospels versus the rest? We know that the Gospels get particular focus during Advent and Easter, but what about the rest of the time? While we claim to be followers of Jesus, we tend to be students of Paul; we tend to study Paul's letters more than the writings that relate directly to Jesus's life—the Gospels. When we do invest ourselves in the Gospels, is it for the purpose of discipleship—that is, are we reading to understand more fully what it means to imitate Jesus? Or do we tend to focus more on his birth and death while ignoring the middle part of his life?

It would be interesting to conduct a survey of a large number of evangelical Christians to find out which passages actually determine their theological positions. What passages are they most familiar with? Which ones do they know least well? What are the more popular Gospel passages—the ones I suggest above, or others? What passages from the epistles are best known? And, of course, the biggest questions of all: what theological conclusions are they inclined to draw based upon the passages most familiar to them? And what are they missing from the call of God upon their lives as a result? As we all know, just about any theological position can be drawn from Scripture if the focus is narrow enough. What theological positions, though, are likely to emerge if we have genuinely invested ourselves in the Bible as a whole? Dietrich Bonhoeffer once commented that he had read through the entire Hebrew Bible two and a half times in the space of a month while he was in prison. He went on to say that it was amazing what he began to see once immersed in Scripture to that degree. The subtle references between books and passages became clearer, as well as the unity of Scripture around the acts of God.

To give only one example from popular Christianity in the latter parts of the twentieth and early parts of the twenty-first centuries, consider the fascination with what are often considered to be the "apocalyptic" writings. Many Christians have been drawn into speculation about the end of the world, and they invest themselves heavily in the study of the book of Revelation, the book of Daniel, and a select portion of the Hebrew prophets. The result has been a virtual mountain of books written in attempt to interpret these writings in order to be able to predict contemporary events. Who is the antichrist? Is he alive today? Who are the various nations referred to in these books? Most importantly, where are we on the time line that concludes with the end of the world? By reading the Bible in a particular way, these authors have concluded that they can discern the true meaning of these writings and tell us how history will unfold. That no one has done a particularly good job of this has hardly deterred others from entering the fray. However, there is a school of thought that argues these writings are not about the future as much as they were about the days in which the writers lived. We need not get into that debate, but we do need to note that by taking a particular method for reading Scripture and by adopting certain favorite passages, people can come to very different conclusions.

The most important point for our discussions is the recognition that most of us hold the view of Christian faith we do because of a small handful of favorite biblical texts. This small handful of texts becomes the lens through which everything is understood. Our goal as serious students of Scripture should be to increase our grasp of the overarching biblical story by constantly expanding our familiarity with the Bible. Many people reach adulthood with perspectives that have been dictated by theologies derived from a small group of biblical texts.

While an exhaustive study of the biblical narrative is beyond the scope of this book, we can begin the task of developing a holistic picture of the type of life God expects of us by starting at the beginning (Genesis) and continuing through to the end (Revelation), with stops at various places to provide a vision of the life of the community that should guide us theopolitically. What follows is neither a random selection of passages nor a set of prooftexts. Rather it is an attempt to gather a rich and broad set of representative texts that paint a picture of how we are to live together. This will be a basis for making judgments about what constitutes a "Christian view" of the questions at hand. Other passages could be considered as well. Let us turn our attention now to several biblical vignettes intended to answer the question of what a public life that pleases God might look like.

Genesis 1:26–28

This passage comes toward the end of the creation narrative of Genesis 1 and explicitly provides the short account of the creation of humanity (the longer account is found in Genesis 2). Here we are given some very important information about God's creation of humans. First, the text indicates that God created man and woman in his own image. How this is to be understood has been debated. I have argued that we are to understand this as a profound affirmation of our having been created as persons for relationship because we are created in the image of a God who is community. Second, God instructs humans to be fruitful and to spread throughout the world God has created. Third, and of particular importance for our discussions here, God instructs his human creatures to exercise authority over the world and its creatures. In effect, God indicates that he intends for the humans he has created to act as his *regents* in the world, to be responsible to him for tending to the earth and its creatures. Often the translations indicate that God has given "dominion" to humanity. But we have to be very careful how we take this term. In our twenty-first century context, the term "dominion" has come to carry with it the connotations of sovereign authority, control, or domination. It is clear, however, from the rest of Scripture that God intends this more in the sense of exercising stewardship and care for the world. God is not saying, "The world is yours, do with it what you want." Unfortunately, some have taken it this way and think that humans have the right to exploit the earth as they see fit. In reality, humans are given both *authority* and *responsibility*.

The life that pleases God, then, involves human stewardship of God's good creation. The responsibilities that attend this assignment must be kept in mind as we argue for this or that public policy. Simply leaving it for the market to decide how to balance care for the earth against profits too easily sets aside the concerns of the vast majority for whom the world is created. Furthermore, we must realize that part of our obligation to exercise stewardship over the earth is the responsibility to leave the creation in better shape for those who follow us. God does not intend for us to live as if we were going to be the last to live on the earth. Part of our obligation of stewardship involves looking forward to subsequent generations.

Genesis 12

In the third verse of this chapter, God calls Abram (later Abraham) to come out from among his people to another place and to another role. He is to become the father of a great people, and these people will become the bearers of the Messiah. Unfortunately, too often we miss an important aspect of Abraham's call, namely that he is being blessed in order to be a blessing. Abraham is not merely the recipient of blessing, one who benefits without any expectations placed upon him. Instead he is to be God's channel of blessing to the rest of humanity. This is the earliest occurrence of a recurring theme within Scripture, namely the theme of receiving blessing in order to serve others. Normally we view the gifts and skills that we have as ours to use as we please. Further, we view the things we come to own through the use of those gifts and skills as things that we have earned and deserve. Scripture, however, reminds us that these things all come to us from God and thus that we are accountable to him for how we use them.

One of the complexities that arises when one tries to take seriously the obligation to use one's blessings to benefit others is trying to determine the appropriate boundaries for such generosity. For example, do parents give away so much that their own children are put in jeopardy? I seriously doubt that this is what God has in mind. However, we have to deal with our human tendency to answer the question "How much is enough?" with "Just a little bit more." At the very least, the injunction to use our blessings in service of others is intended to remind us of our obligations to ease the suffering of the poor and those otherwise on the margins. This is a continual concern that God expresses, and thus embodying generosity is a central aspect of the life that pleases God.

Exodus 19

Continuing in a similar but somewhat different theme, consider verses 5–6 of Exodus 19:

"Now if you obey me fully and keep my covenant, then out of all
nations you will be my treasured possession. Although the whole
earth is mine, you will be for me a kingdom of priests and a holy
nation." These are the words you are to speak to the Israelites. (NIV)

At first glance, this passage seems to be mostly about God's
call to the descendants of Abraham to be his people. While this
is true, the common translations lead us to miss a very important point. In fact, the translations often obscure the connection
between the ideas of blessing and serving as priests. The sentiment expressed in the verse could better be interpreted, "Since
the whole world is created for relationship with me (God), I call
you to be the ministers of my grace to the world." Those called
by God are called for the sake of others.[1] What is it that priests
do? They mediate God's grace to people. By calling his chosen
people a priestly kingdom, God affirms the role of the nation
of Israel to serve as the agents of his blessing to the rest of the
world. They are not to hold or to hoard blessings but to release
them. Too easily the calling to be God's chosen can lead us to
believe we are blessed for our own sakes rather than for the sake
of the world. However, this reverses God's intent.

Some have argued that the failure of Israel to live out God's
expectations was primarily a failure to understand the purpose
of their calling with regard to this particular point. Likewise,
perhaps the primary point missed by contemporary Christians
is the failure to realize the "for the nations" aspect of our service
to God. Too easily we allow our own self-interests to obscure our
obligations to those on the margins.

Exodus 20

In this chapter we find the succinct set of instructions God provides to his people regarding how they are supposed to live out

their day-to-day lives. We call them the Ten Commandments. If one looks closely at the nature of these commandments, one finds that they divide into two broad categories. The first four deal with the human relationship with God—we are not to worship any other god, not to misuse God's name, and so forth. The second six deal with the relationships between humans—we are not to steal, murder, lie, and so on. This way of dividing the commandments recalls Jesus's answer to the question about the greatest commandment. He says that we are to love God with our whole being and to love our neighbors as ourselves. In a sense, then, Jesus's answer in the Gospels is a pair of generalizations derived from the more specific content of the Ten Commandments. These provide a set of instructions for constructing our life together in a way that is pleasing to God.

Interestingly, modern liberal democracies (and other governmental forms as well, but we focus primarily upon forms employed by the United States because they have relegated religion to private life) give very little attention to the first part of the commandments—those dealing with God. In fact, in most modern societies one need not even believe in God at all much less worry about idolatry. I will argue, generally in agreement with John Locke (though I will disagree with him at several points), that we should make provision for citizens to practice religion as they choose.[2]

This means that we should minimize obstacles to religious expression—with the exception, of course, of those religious practices that overtly harm people—while not making one religion the "state religion." The second part of the commandments is overwhelmingly understood to set out important moral distinctions, but not all of them are embodied in the laws of the state. For example, while adultery is viewed as immoral, we do not have laws against it. On the other hand, we readily agree that both murder and robbery are to be outlawed. When we draw our conclusions at the end of the chapter, we will return to the Ten Commandments as part of a discussion about the extent to which the moral code is to be embodied in law. At the very least, we should put in place public policies and institutions that allow citizens to worship according to the dictates of their own conscience and express the healthy interactions that would result from following the command to love our neighbor as ourselves.

Exodus 22

> If you lend money to my people, to the poor among you, you shall not deal with them as a creditor; you shall not exact interest from them. If you take your neighbor's cloak in pawn, you shall restore it before the sun goes down; for it may be your neighbor's only clothing to use as cover; in what else shall that person sleep? And if your neighbor cries out to me, I will listen, for I am compassionate. (vv. 25–27)

This particular passage is very interesting and deserves our attention on at least three different levels. While we cannot imagine a world in which money is lent without interest, it seems that God certainly can imagine it. This is consistent with the earlier observations that God expects us to use our blessings to benefit others. Rather than using our resources to benefit ourselves (by charging for the use of money), we are to use our resources for the benefit of others. Part of the extraordinary care God intends for the poor and those otherwise on the margins is exemplified in this instruction.

Note the second expectation God has for an economy that meets his intentions. Clearly, God's expectation that care for the poor be built into the laws of the land is evident in the collateral laws given here. When a poor person gives a cloak in pledge for a loan, God instructs the lender to return the cloak at sunset since the poor person will not likely have another means of keeping warm at night. God puts the care of the poor first, even above profits. Collateral is acceptable, but the potential risk to the needy person outweighs the risk to the capital lent.

Finally, notice that God does not take lightly the failure to heed this command—those who should choose to disobey it can expect that God will hear the needy when they cry out to God. The particularly vulnerable condition of the poor makes them a group to which God seems especially attentive. Our own selfishness often precludes our proper attention to the poor, so God assumes the role of their advocate. Yet this does not let us off the hook. We are expected to use our blessings to benefit others.

Leviticus 19

As we noted previously, an important concept in discussing God's nature is the concept of holiness. We noted already that holiness is often defined negatively within Christian circles, that is, by identifying a list of things that one does not do. Too often Christians feel they have satisfied the call to holiness if they do not, for example, engage in illicit sex or drug abuse. To think of holiness in this way, though, does not do justice to the fact that holiness is a relational concept. Consider the first half of Leviticus 19:

> The LORD spoke to Moses, saying: Speak to all the congregation of the people of Israel and say to them: You shall be holy, for I the LORD your God am holy. You shall each revere your mother and father, and you shall keep my sabbaths: I am the LORD your God. Do not turn to idols or make cast images for yourselves: I am the LORD your God. When you offer a sacrifice of well-being to the LORD, offer it in such a way that it is acceptable in your behalf. It shall be eaten on the same day you offer it, or on the next day; and

anything left over until the third day shall be consumed in fire. If it is eaten at all on the third day, it is an abomination; it will not be acceptable. All who eat it shall be subject to punishment, because they have profaned what is holy to the LORD; and any such person shall be cut off from the people. When you reap the harvest of your land, you shall not reap to the very edges of your field, or gather the gleanings of your harvest. You shall not strip your vineyard bare, or gather the fallen grapes of your vineyard; you shall leave them for the poor and the alien: I am the LORD your God.

You shall not steal; you shall not deal falsely; and you shall not lie to one another. And you shall not swear falsely by my name, profaning the name of your God: I am the LORD. You shall not defraud your neighbor; you shall not steal; and you shall not keep for yourself the wages of a laborer until morning. You shall not revile the deaf or put a stumbling block before the blind; you shall fear your God: I am the LORD. You shall not render an unjust judgment; you shall not be partial to the poor or defer to the great: with justice you shall judge your neighbor. You shall not go around as a slanderer among your people, and you shall not profit by the blood of your neighbor: I am the LORD. You shall not hate in your heart anyone of your kin; you shall reprove your neighbor, or you will incur guilt yourself. You shall not take vengeance or bear a grudge against any of your people, but you shall love your neighbor as yourself: I am the LORD.

There are two important points to take from this passage. First, notice how frequently the simple affirmation "I am the Lord" appears. In each case, the intent of the text is to suggest once again the affirmation that it is their God who is speaking and that God expects them to imitate his own holiness. Second, notice the profoundly relational content of the various commands. In every case, this twofold notion appears: God's holiness is to be imitated by his people, and imitating God's holiness means to live in the sorts of relationships implied by the commands. And a good many of the issues explicitly raised are directly related to the very sorts of concerns that we identify as "social justice."

Notice also the command not to show partiality to any in administering the law (v. 15). At first glance, we might wonder about this. Does not God show an extra special degree of care for those who are poor or otherwise on the margins? Why, then, this concern that partiality not be shown to either poor or rich? God intends for care for the poor and marginalized to be administered impartially through laws that are formulated with them in mind. For example, recall the collateral laws we just examined. In essence, God demands that the laws themselves be structured to assure that what we would call "social justice" is properly addressed. When this is so, we can simply be satisfied to "treat all equally under the law."

Leviticus 25

The periodic economic leveling known as the Years of Jubilee are described in some detail in this chapter. Since we discussed this previously, we need only summarize here. Every fifty years, all properties were to be returned to their ancestral owners. In fact, God describes the sale of property not so much as a sale of property but rather like renting the use of the land. We have discussed how this law, commanded by God, seemed intended to prevent the rise of a permanently dispossessed class of people. By returning the ancestral land to their families every fifty years, families, even those who fall into trouble of one sort or another, are not to become long-term victims of their misfortune. Rather, they are to be restored.

Deuteronomy 15

This chapter begins by providing the details for the Years of Release wherein those who are in debt to their neighbor are to be forgiven their debts. God grants an exception for those who are not members of the community, but for all others the debts that have been incurred are to be forgiven every seven years. Notice that God takes this so seriously that he warns against those who would entertain the thought of withholding from those who would borrow in the sixth year. If one has the resources, one is to lend them, even though the debts will be forgiven in the subsequent year. To fail to lend under these conditions is to incur guilt before God.

> There will, however, be no one in need among you, because the LORD is sure to bless you in the land that the LORD your God is giving you as a possession to occupy, if only you will obey the LORD your God by diligently observing this entire commandment that I command you today. (vv. 4–5)

God does not give these commands to hold one's material goods loosely and to engage in years of debt remission for abstract reasons. Rather, God intends for there to be no poor among his people. Notice the conditional statement in verse 5: *if* the people will obey God on these points, *the result will be* that there will be no poor. There will be enough to meet the needs of all *as long as* God's commands against hoarding are observed. To the extent we fail to observe these commands and insist on some having excess, we will fail to meet God's intentions and there will, in fact, be poor among us. (See the section on Matthew 26 on page 105 for more on this subject.)

Deuteronomy 17

This particularly interesting chapter foresees the day in which the Israelites will want to have a king. The insistence by the Israelites later in the book of Samuel to have a king to rule over them is often characterized as a rejection of God. However, if we put that passage within the context of this particular chapter, we come to a somewhat different conclusion. It seems that the issue God was concerned about was not having a king per se but rather the insistence by the people that they have a king *like those the other nations had*. These other nations had a king whose strength and authority were rooted in the typical power paradigms in which we humans normally traffic. God's objection was to the manner in which the king would embody his rule. The rejection of God was most fundamentally the rejection of the idea that he knows best.

In Deuteronomy 17, there are three specific characteristics of a king who is satisfactory to God. At first, each of these might sound a little strange to us. Upon closer examination, we can see that each is related to some aspect of what it meant to be a king in the ancient Near East. First, the king that Israel would have was not to gather horses. Horses were the ancient Near Eastern equivalent of the B-1 bomber: fighting on horseback was the state of the art in contemporary weaponry. To be instructed not to hoard horses was to be instructed not to trust in one's own military might or cleverness.

Second, the king was instructed not to intermarry with those around him. At first, this seems likely to be about racial purity. However, the means of forming strategic alliances in the ancient Near East was through intermarrying. God is telling us that we are not to trust our own cleverness and strategies in protecting ourselves.

Finally, the king was not to spend time building a great economic empire. To do so would certainly mean falling prey to trusting in one's economic might as a means of exerting power over others. In short, each of these three points constitutes ways in which we trust in our own cleverness to protect ourselves against the threats that inhabit our world as humans. The biblical view of a king (only finally and fully to be realized in Jesus) is very different from our normal conceptions of kingship and of the power that national leaders wield.

Deuteronomy 24:14–22

> You shall not withhold the wages of poor and needy laborers, whether other Israelites or aliens who reside in your land in one of your towns. You shall pay them their wages daily before sunset, because they are poor and their livelihood depends on them; otherwise they might cry to the Lord against you, and you would incur guilt. Parents shall not be put to death for their children, nor shall children be put to death for their parents; only for their own crimes may persons be put to death. You shall not deprive a resident alien or an orphan of justice; you shall not take a widow's garment in pledge. Remember that you were a slave in Egypt and the Lord your God redeemed you from there; therefore I command you to do this. When you reap your harvest in your field and forget a sheaf in the field, you shall not go back to get it; it shall be left for the alien, the orphan, and the widow, so that the Lord your God may bless you in all your undertakings. When you beat your olive trees, do not strip what is left; it shall be for the alien, the orphan, and the widow. When you gather the grapes of your vineyard, do not glean what is left; it shall be for the alien, the orphan, and the widow. Remember that you were a slave in the land of Egypt; therefore I am commanding you to do this.

First, God commands that employers are to pay their workers immediately. Running a business on the float from laborers' wages is hardly a new idea, and it is one that God finds unacceptable. Second, God does not allow people to be punished in the stead of others. All are to be accountable for their own crimes and wrongdoing. Third, even resident aliens in the land are to be treated justly and fairly. It is interesting that God connects this command with a reminder of the Israelites' past status as slaves in the land of Egypt. Since they knew what it was like to be treated unjustly, they are not to repeat this treatment with resident aliens in their own land. Fourth, God explicitly commands that farmers and vineyard owners are not to maximize profits. Again God places people and their well-being over attempts to squeeze every last cent out of the fields. To the contrary, the fields were to be left with some pickings for the poor, the widow, and the orphan.

Each of these commands given by God as to be part of the Israelites' law. If followed, the commands were intended to create an environment in which "there would be no poor" among God's people. Contrary to our contemporary setting in which we too easily blame the poor for their plight, God clearly and unequivocally places the responsibility for caring for the poor directly on the shoulders of those who are in control and well-off.

Psalms and Proverbs

Numerous verses and passages in the Wisdom books deal with God's particular concern for the poor. You might take a few hours to sit down and read through them in their entirety in order to get a grasp on the extent to which the notions we have been discussing permeate these books. We will list just a few here with little or no commentary.

"Because the poor are despoiled, because the needy groan, I will now rise up," says the LORD; "I will place them in the safety for which they long." (Ps. 12:5)

Happy are those who consider the poor; the LORD delivers them in the day of trouble. (Ps. 41:1)

For he delivers the needy when they call, the poor and those who have no helper. (Ps. 72:12)

They have distributed freely, they have given to the poor; their righteousness endures forever; their horn is exalted in honor. (Ps. 112:9)

I know that the LORD maintains the cause of the needy, and executes justice for the poor. (Ps. 140:12)

The field of the poor may yield much food, but it is swept away through injustice. (Prov. 13:23)

Those who mock the poor insult their Maker; those who are glad at calamity will not go unpunished. (Prov. 17:5)

Whoever is kind to the poor lends to the LORD, and will be repaid in full. (Prov. 19:17)

If you close your ear to the cry of the poor, you will cry out and not be heard. (Prov. 21:13)

Whoever gives to the poor will lack nothing, but one who turns a blind eye will get many a curse. (Prov. 28:27)

These passages (and there are many more like them) provide important wisdom regarding the manner in which God expects us to deal with the poor or those otherwise on the margins of our societies. As we have said all along, however, these passages are not presented to prove anything as much as they are to illumine us to God's concerns, which we should embody in our imitation of God. What would it look like to take this vision seriously and to seek to structure society in ways that empower and reward this way of being?

Isaiah 10

At the beginning of this chapter, the prophet Isaiah explicitly recognizes that unjust governmental systems can make a contribution to the plight of the poor. Consider the first two verses:

> Ah, you who make iniquitous decrees, who write oppressive statutes, to turn aside the needy from justice and to rob the poor of my people of their right, that widows may be your spoil, and that you may make the orphans your prey! (vv. 1–2)

In this particular translation, the reference is made to those who make decrees (explicitly, of course, iniquitous ones). In other translations, the term "legislators" is used. Whichever term a translation uses, we should note that these warnings are not about making laws that harm the poor and the oppressed. Rather, the text implies that there is a temptation on the part of lawmakers to use their powers of legislation to slant the playing field in ways that "rob the poor of their *right*" (emphasis added) and that exploit the widows and orphans. These two groups of citizens are the ones that are particularly vulnerable because they do not have ready access to the levers of power that control the nation. In addition, widows and orphans were in biblical times and are still two groups that are consistently at risk because they are often unable to provide for themselves when they are not under the protection of others. As a consequence, God says those who make laws have to be especially attentive to the plight of these groups in order to assure their protection.

There are three important points we should infer from this text. First, there is no indication that making laws, or legislating, is inherently either evil or outside of divine intention. Laws are good things, ordained by God to help order and structure our common lives, as long as the laws are just and empower the kinds of communities God intends. Second, it follows that God's people are to be concerned about the sorts of laws that a given culture chooses to embody its priorities and values. Hence, engaging in legislation, either directly or indirectly, is both necessary and good. Third, this passage explicitly recognizes the possibility of institutional evil—evil that is built into the system of laws governing a particular society. This implies an obligation to do all that we can to ensure that this system does not oppress those most vulnerable in society (or anyone else for that matter).

Jeremiah 29

John Howard Yoder has an interesting take on the first several verses of this chapter. We noted earlier that as part of his commission to the first humans, God instructs them to spread out over the earth. They are "to be fruitful and multiply" as well as to exercise stewardship over creation. In the Babel accounts, God intervenes to disperse his people to serve his intentions and to reach out to the world. One of the besetting sins of ancient Israel was its tendency to focus on its role as the chosen people to the point of missing the call to serve as ministers of God's grace to the rest of the world. Yoder suggests that the dispersion of the Israelites at the Babylonian exile was a way of accomplishing the scattering of his people that God had intended they undertake on their own.[3] We get comfortable in our own places (Babel, Israel, or wherever "here" is) and resist moving out as God instructs. Occasionally, he intervenes and takes things into his own hands.

If this interpretation is correct, then we see an interesting movement in this passage from earlier instructions God gave to the people. While God was teaching them about himself and what it meant to be God's people, he had instructed them not to intermarry. Now that they are scattered into other countries, however, God allows marrying with the locals even though they are not Israelites. God tells them, in essence, that in their role as agents of God's grace in the world, they are now to intermarry and to participate in the life of the cities where they dwell. Their good is now connected with the good of the local people. There is no risk of using these relationships for strategic alliances since the Israelites are now powerless. Rather, now the goal is to more closely bind together God's chosen people with those who have been enemies to Israel.

Ezekiel 16

This is an important passage because it adds some context to the popular interpretations of the destruction of Sodom. As a whole, this section of Ezekiel focuses on judgment for Jerusalem for failing to live up to God's expectations. In verse 48, God identifies the similarity between the sins of contemporary Jerusalem and those for which Sodom was destroyed. What are they? Those in Sodom were guilty of being sated with food while not hearing the cry of the needy. In short, they had failed to take seriously the concern for those who were poor and instead had become selfish and greedy.

Once we place the destruction of Sodom within its historical time frame, the passage becomes all the more striking. First, it is highly significant that these judgments are made against a city-state that was not a part of the chosen people of God. In other words, Sodom was not the recipient of special instruction from God indicating the obligation to hear the cry of the needy. Yet it is still held accountable. Care for the needy should be a matter of common sense. Second, if we consider that the Sodom story occurs in the book of Genesis, we will notice that not even Israel had yet been given God's law. In fact, the law would not be given for another four centuries. God takes the call to social justice to be sufficiently evident that the punishment meted out to Sodom could be seen as just.

One final note worth considering: the city of Sodom was completely destroyed, which suggests that the failure was not merely a failure of personal charity but rather a complete breakdown in society's communal obligations to tend to those who were most vulnerable. In other words, the obligations we have discussed here are not merely obligations that we incur as individuals but also, and perhaps more preeminently, obligations that we incur as communities. Just as there are both personal and institutional expectations to live up to, there are personal and institutional evils to be avoided. This only amplifies the inferences we drew from the passage in Isaiah relating to the establishment of just legislation. Legislation can serve the divine agenda, or it can become an enemy to it. It is our job as Christians to advocate for the former.[4]

Amos 2

The entire book of Amos is enlightening in that it expresses God's judgment on a ruling class that has lost sight of its obligations to the public it serves. In other words, the book of Amos embodies a powerful critique of public institutions that have, in a very real sense, run amock. How so? Let us consider a short passage from the second chapter that captures a consistent theme that runs throughout Amos. Consider verses 6–8:

> Thus says the LORD: For three transgressions of Israel, and for four, I will not revoke the punishment; because they sell the righteous for silver, and the needy for a pair of sandals, they who trample the head of the poor into the dust of the earth, and push the afflicted out of the way; father and son go in to the same girl, so that my

holy name is profaned; they lay themselves down beside every altar on garments taken in pledge; and in the house of their God they drink wine bought with fines they imposed.

Notice the corruption of the ruling class. First, they "sell the righteous for silver." In other words, they are quite happy to get rid of the righteous ones in their community—perhaps out of pure greed, perhaps because the righteous remind them of their own perversity. Whatever the reason, they value riches, represented here by "silver," more than they value righteousness. The poor and marginalized are of no concern to these rulers—they readily exploit them to serve their own appetites. Afterward, those whom they have exploited and afflicted are pushed out of sight. Sexual impropriety is practiced here as well, which indicates that the breakdown involves both public and private morality. Note in particular the reference to garments taken in pledge but used for the ease of these perverse rulers. Recall that when taken in pledge from the poor, garments were to be returned at the end of the day. As God noted, those garments might be all that stands between that poor person and the elements. Here the rulers have perverted those laws to make themselves comfortable. Finally, these rulers have imposed fines on their people in order to feed their own thirst for wine. The very fees that should be used to further the common good have been redirected for the luxury of the ruling class.

Once again, we see the institutional evil that can so easily be connected with our systems of governance. To suggest that Christians should not speak prophetically to governments that fail to pass legislation that takes seriously the need to care for the poor and needy is to miss the message of Amos. We are to speak truth to those in power as followers and imitators of the God of Abraham, Isaac, and Jacob in order to prevent the exploitation of society's vulnerable members. We must keep in mind the fact that to be quiet in the midst of perverse societal structures is to effectively participate in the exploitation of those on the margins. We become either a part of the release of oppression and injustice or we become complicit in allowing those unjust structures to stand.

Micah 6

This passage is a classic in social justice circles as it indicates what God expects of us: do justice, love kindness, and walk humbly with God. The most forceful verses are 6–8:

> "With what shall I come before the LORD, and bow myself before God on high? Shall I come before him with burnt offerings, with calves a year old? Will the LORD be pleased with thousands of rams, with ten thousands of rivers of oil? Shall I give my firstborn for my transgression, the fruit of my body for the sin of my soul?" He has told you, O mortal, what is good; and what does the LORD require of you but to do justice, and to love kindness, and to walk humbly with your God?

Notice the anguish with which the writer asks his questions. How will I please God? How will I live in accord with his expectations? And when I do not, how shall I make my relationship with God right again? The questioning is sprinkled with ideas about the possible sacrifices one might offer—calves, thousands of rams, rivers of oil, even a firstborn child. What will it take to live up to the awful expectations of God? And when we do not live up to them, what will it take to make things right?

The answer seems to be yet another way of invoking the two great commandments—to love God and to love neighbor. First, we must engage in just acts. What else can this mean but that we are to interact with those around us in just and fair ways?

Second, we are to "love kindness." Again, toward whom are we to show loving kindness? Those with whom we come in contact. Both of these parts have as their focus interpersonal relationships between humans. The last of the three statements captures the other half of the great commandments, namely, relationship to God. This particular passage puts this very strongly, but in terms we might not expect. We are to "walk with" God and to do this in a humble fashion. Could we connect these by suggesting that they cannot be undertaken apart from each other? That is, can we really walk with God humbly if we do not love mercy and act justly? I do not think so. Loving God and loving our neighbors are at the center of Micah's message.

Matthew 5–7

Of all the passages attributed to Jesus in the Gospels, the Sermon on the Mount is by far the longest. Within the space of these three chapters early in Matthew, Jesus comments on a wide range of moral and ethical issues. In these few chapters, Jesus paints a picture of the life that pleases God, from the Beatitudes in chapter 5 to the comparison of those who follow these teachings to a man who built his house upon a solid rock (rather than on shifting sand, the result of ignoring Jesus's teachings).

One of the ongoing debates about the Sermon on the Mount has to do with the extent to which it is to be taken literally. For example, are we really supposed to take literally the Beatitudes, which seem to turn our normal way of understanding the world upside down? The scribes and the Pharisees were the religious people of the day; what does it mean to demand a level of righteousness that exceeds that of the religious experts? Are we really supposed to simply answer all questions with a simple yes or no? Is it really the case that no oaths are allowed? Does God seriously expect us to turn the other cheek and genuinely love our enemies? And later: must we be perfect as our heavenly Father is perfect? The sheer force of these sorts of injunctions has not been lost on many. The interpretation often suggested for the Sermon on the Mount is that these are the perfections expected of us "in the next life," or these are "councils of perfection" required of the "spiritually adept" rather than your average believer. Or, equally problematic, they are interpreted to mean our "inner motivations." The common thread in all of these interpretations is an attempt to hold ourselves to a lower standard than that to which the Sermon actually calls us.

Why not simply accept that these injunctions actually embody God's expectations for us? Mark Twain once famously remarked that it was not those parts of the Bible that he did not understand that caused him concerns but rather the parts that he did. If we are actually expected to live up to those parts we understand, Twain implied, we would have to adopt a way of living far out of touch with our normal inclinations. But what is Jesus asking in the Sermon that we have not seen already in our review of Scripture? If anything, he merely begins to give intensity and specificity to the idea that we are to put the interests of others above our own. I commend you to stop and take the time to read through this powerful expression of the life that pleases God and to reflect on how that relates to how we are to structure our life together.

Matthew 25

The last sixteen verses of this chapter are often referred to as the "pericope of the great judgment." Here Jesus explains what it will be like to finally have to give to God an account of our lives. He nicely summarizes the life that pleases God. Tom Sine once started a chapel sermon by asking the students how well they would expect to do on a final exam if they were given the questions in advance. All agreed that knowing the questions in advance should result in making an A. The giggles gave way to reflection when he observed that these few verses constitute our "final exam" before God.

What kinds of things are included in this exam? Jesus recites the same list of activities for both groups, but only one group has done them.

> I was hungry and you gave me food, I was thirsty and you gave me something to drink, I was a stranger and you welcomed me, I was naked and you gave me clothing, I was sick and you took care of me, I was in prison and you visited me. (vv. 35–36)

Interestingly, the response that both groups give is identical—they ask when they have seen Jesus and either done or not done these things. Then comes the surprising transference: they have done these things to him to the extent they have done them to "the least of these." By serving others with self-giving love, we are serving our Lord himself. It has often been suggested that we should judge the success or failure of our systems of governance by how well "the least of these" are doing. Of course, we cannot directly infer specific public policies from this, but we can begin to understand the priority God gives to caring for the least of these.

Matthew 26

Matthew 26:11 is often cited in amateur debate about how Christians are to be concerned about the plight of the poor. In this verse, Jesus indicates that we will always have the poor among us. Some take this to mean that there is an inevitability about the presence of the poor that makes it futile for us to become too concerned about getting rid of poverty. Why waste time trying to cure a problem that Jesus says will not be cured? I have even had discussion partners go so far as to suggest that trying to cure poverty is somehow going against Jesus's teaching. They seem to see Jesus's descriptive comments as proscriptive, thus any effort to solve the problem of poverty undermines Jesus's counsel. This badly misses the point. According to Deuteronomy, there should be no poor among God's people.

It is essential that we note the broader context within which this statement is situated. Just before Jesus's betrayal and execution, a woman anoints Jesus with expensive oil. The disciples begin to grumble about whether it would have been a better use of her money to use it to feed the poor instead. But Jesus reminds the disciples that the woman's act serves to prepare him for the events to come. Jesus might have meant three things by observing that the poor would always be among them. First, he might simply be making an observation about human nature without intending to make any particular judgments. I think this is unlikely, but it is possible. Second, he might be making an observation about the intended social location of his followers, that is, affirming the role of the followers of Jesus in embodying his presence *with* the poor after he has gone. Finally, he might be implying a rather harsh judgment, namely, that there will always be poor among us because we are too selfish to take the steps necessary to prevent it. This would make sense and would make clear how far we are from the intentions of Deuteronomy 15. Whatever the case, Jesus is certainly not giving his followers an excuse to do nothing to care for the poor.

Luke 4

This chapter of Luke's Gospel covers a number of important events. It begins with Jesus fasting in the desert for forty days and facing the devil to deal with those three great temptations we know so well. The chapter concludes with a couple of healings—a demon exorcism in the synagogue and the healing of Peter's mother-in-law. Sandwiched between these accounts is the report of Jesus's attending a synagogue on the Sabbath. Verses 16–21 give us the details:

> When he came to Nazareth, where he had been brought up, he went to the synagogue on the sabbath day, as was his custom. He stood up to read, and the scroll of the prophet Isaiah was given to him. He unrolled the scroll and found the place where it was written: "The Spirit of the LORD is upon me, because he has anointed me to bring good news to the poor. He has sent me to proclaim release to the captives and recovery of sight to the blind, to let the oppressed go free, to proclaim the year of the LORD's favor." And he rolled up the scroll, gave it back to the attendant, and sat down. The eyes of all in the synagogue were fixed on him. Then he began to say to them, "Today this scripture has been fulfilled in your hearing."

It is interesting that the reading of the day, from Isaiah, contained these particular words. After reading the Scripture, Jesus indicates that these words from the prophet Isaiah are to be understood as being embodied in his own ministry. In fact, one might characterize the contents of that reading from Isaiah as Jesus's "mission statement." Jesus identifies his mission as declaring good news for the poor, freeing the oppressed, and bringing release to the captives and sight to the blind. As heirs of Jesus's ministry, we are to take up this mission as our own. We too are to seek to free those who are held captive by sin—whether that be the sin of their own personal choosing or the sinful structures of our society that enslave and imprison them. In this way, we become participants in announcing and embodying the Good

News. Any news that does not aim toward this end cannot genuinely be considered the Good News of the gospel.

Luke 10

Much of what we have discussed so far reinforces the biblical call to elevate the needs of others above our own and to embody lives of self-giving love. We have already seen in the Sermon on the Mount that the "other" to whom we are to extend self-giving love includes even our enemies. The parable of the Good Samaritan once again draws our attention to the question, Who is the other I am to love and to serve?

An exchange between Jesus and a lawyer begins in verse 25. The first question asked is, "What must I do to inherit eternal life?" The lawyer does not mince words; he simply wants to know what sorts of things are required of those who seek to live in God's presence. Jesus responds by asking him how he reads "the law." The lawyer responds by citing the two great commandments—love God with all your being and your neighbor as yourself. Jesus approves of the answer, but then the lawyer asks another question: "Who is my neighbor?" The answer, told in the form of a parable, is rather shocking.

In the parable, a Jewish man is robbed and beaten, and fellow Jews do not stop to help him. The one who does stop is a Samaritan. Samaritans were viewed as half-breeds unworthy of being counted among God's people. Yet this Samaritan embodies the self-giving love God expects of his followers while the injured man's Jewish fellows do not. It is the reviled Samaritan who ends up treating the Jewish man as a neighbor, and Jesus tells the lawyer to do the same. To the question, "Who is my neighbor?" Jesus answers, "The one you are least likely to love." We should not be surprised, for the Sermon on the Mount has already instructed us that we fail to imitate the love of God if we love only our friends. The parable of the Good Samaritan reminds us that there are no boundaries involved in loving others.

Luke 12

The parable of the rich fool is particularly challenging to our contemporary way of understanding what constitutes the good life. Just prior to this parable, a man asks Jesus to instruct his brother to divide their family inheritance fairly. Jesus gives three responses. First, Jesus indicates that he has no role to play in adjudicating their family dispute. Next, he gives a somewhat surprising response: "Take care! Be on your guard against all kinds of greed; for one's life does not consist in the abundance of possessions."

Third and finally, he proceeds to tell the parable of the rich fool:

> Then he told them a parable: "The land of a rich man produced abundantly. And he thought to himself, 'What should I do, for I have no place to store my crops?' Then he said, 'I will do this: I will pull down my barns and build larger ones, and there I will store all my grain and my goods. And I will say to my soul, Soul, you have ample goods laid up for many years; relax, eat, drink, be merry.' But God said to him, 'You fool! This very night your life is being demanded of you. And the things you have prepared, whose will they be?' So it is with those who store up treasures for themselves but are not rich toward God." (vv. 16–21)

A man has worked hard and his crops have done exceptionally well, so he decides to build storehouses, store away his good fortune, and take what we would call early retirement. What is wrong with that? Doesn't our culture tell us that this is exactly what this entrepreneurial and enterprising fellow deserves? Perhaps, but our obligations to each other run much deeper than this man was aware. God gives blessings so that we might bless others. In this case, the man understood this great harvest as the result of his own labors and therefore his personal property. As a result, God says he is a fool, and judgment will follow. Rather than being "rich toward God" and using his resources to benefit others, he stored up his goods for himself.

Passages like this remind us of the ways in which the call of the gospel turns our normal way of thinking upside down. Caring for ourselves first seems intuitively correct to us. Yet the Good News has to be good news for those on the margins, those for whom God consistently shows concern. To imitate God, we must embody that concern at all levels, public and private.

Luke 16

The story of the rich man and Lazarus has a very similar theme to what we just saw in the parable of the rich fool. The rich man in this story does not engage in behavior that can be characterized as proactively evil. He does not injure Lazarus, we have no evidence that he insults him, nor does he try to get Lazarus to go away. Rather, the rich man completely ignores Lazarus. Our culture tells us that the rich man's goods are his own to do with as he pleases. He may voluntarily choose to help Lazarus, but he is under no obligation to do so.

God does not see it this way. The rich man's mortal sin is quite simply that he could have helped Lazarus but did not. Once again, we are reminded of the theme we have seen scattered throughout Scripture—we receive blessing in order to bless others. The obligation that attended the rich man's wealth was to use those riches to ease the suffering of others. He was in a position to be able to help Lazarus, but he turned a blind eye and did nothing. The result is that the rich man ends up in hell while Lazarus ends up in heaven.

One last point is worthy of our attention because the story concludes with one of the characters suffering the ultimate judgment: separation from God. As I noted earlier, I am a firm believer that Scripture teaches what we normally call "salvation by faith." Yet we have to integrate this belief with passages like this as well as that of the Great Judgment from Matthew 25. People who fail to embody the call to self-giving love and to elevating the interests of others consistently find themselves on the unfortunate end of divine judgment. Whatever we may say about how one is initially brought into right relationship with God, Scripture is remarkably clear on the importance of walking in the way that seeks to imitate Jesus. And, as we have seen, there is no realm of human existence—private or public—that is precluded from the sorts of divine expectations we have been discussing.

Philippians 2

As we have said repeatedly, Jesus is the paradigmatic expression of the life that pleases God, thus imitating Jesus is at the core of what it means to be a Christian. In Philippians 2, the extent to which Jesus pours himself out in self-giving love is remarkably expressed in what many believe contains a hymn from the early church. Verse 4 enjoins us to put the interests of others above our own interests, and then we are told how Jesus lived this out in his own life. Let us consider in particular verses 5–11:

> Let the same mind be in you that was in Christ Jesus, who, though he was in the form of God, did not regard equality with God as something to be exploited, but emptied himself, taking the form of a slave, being born in human likeness. And being found in

human form, he humbled himself and became obedient to the point of death even death on a cross. Therefore God also highly exalted him and gave him the name that is above every name, so that at the name of Jesus every knee should bend, in heaven and on earth and under the earth, and every tongue should confess that Jesus Christ is Lord, to the glory of God the Father.

As we have noted, many places in Scripture enjoin us to be imitators of God. In this case, that comes in the form of being told to have the same mind as Jesus—to see things as he did and to make judgments as he did. Jesus of Nazareth is the second person of the Trinity incarnate. If Jesus did not grasp after equality with God, how much more ought we resist the temptation to think too highly of ourselves. Jesus took on the life of a servant—a servant who put the interests of others above his own and who lived his life caring for others. While this is undoubtedly a serious challenge, it is nonetheless part of what it means to be imitators of Christ. Jesus was even willing to die for others—a willing obedience even to the point of death on a cross.

1–2 Corinthians

There are many places we could turn in the epistles, but we will consider only a handful. First, consider these two passages from the letters to the church at Corinth:

> For who sees anything different in you? What do you have that you did not receive? And if you received it, why do you boast as if it were not a gift? (1 Cor. 4:7)

> For if the eagerness is there, the gift is acceptable according to what one has, not according to what one does not have. I do not mean that there should be relief for others and pressure on you, but it is a question of a fair balance between your present abundance

and their need, so that their abundance may be for your need, in order that there may be a fair balance. As it is written, "The one who had much did not have too much, and the one who had little did not have too little." (2 Cor. 8:12–15)

In the first passage, we are reminded that as persons created by God, everything we could ever possess is a gift. Even our health and our physical and mental talents are gifts to us from our Creator. Once we understand this, we are less likely to hold onto things so tightly. Everything is freely given to us, so freely giving from our resources becomes easier.

In the latter passage, we are reminded that God intends for our economic life to be structured in a way that assures that great disparities of wealth are avoided. Please note that the passage does not say that all must have the same amount of wealth; there is room for rewarding hard work. But there is no room for allowing so many to have so little, as is currently the case in the United States and in impoverished parts of the world, where billions live on the equivalent of one dollar per day.

James

The entire letter of James is a reminder that faith and works are to be inextricably combined in the life of the follower of Christ. Those familiar with the life of Martin Luther will remember that Luther referenced the epistle of James as a "right strawy epistle."[5] However, one must consider the context of Luther's day, when the importance of the doctrine of justification by faith was being contested. Consequently, Luther was, shall we say, a little resistant to anything that might shift the emphasis away from that doctrine. However, the context in which we find ourselves is very different. In many circles, the doctrine of justification by faith has been elevated to a place of sole importance in determining

right relationship to God. In *The Cost of Discipleship*, Dietrich
Bonhoeffer criticizes our failure to live out the call to be imitators
of Christ. Bonhoeffer suggests that we have adopted an easy faith
that supports a "cheap grace" that costs us nothing because we
have forgotten the cost incurred by God on our behalf. To be a
disciple involves engaging in self-denial and bearing one's cross.[6]

I would commend the entire epistle of James (all five chapters
can be read in minutes) to the readers so that they might get a
fuller sense of the challenges James sets before us. Let us look at
just a few examples.

> Religion that is pure and undefiled before God, the Father, is
> this: to care for orphans and widows in their distress, and to keep
> oneself unstained by the world. (1:27)

> What good is it, my brothers and sisters, if you say you have faith
> but do not have works? Can faith save you? If a brother or sister
> is naked and lacks daily food, and one of you says to them, "Go
> in peace; keep warm and eat your fill," and yet you do not supply
> their bodily needs, what is the good of that? So faith by itself, if it
> has no works, is dead. But someone will say, "You have faith and
> I have works." Show me your faith apart from your works, and I
> by my works will show you my faith. You believe that God is one;
> you do well. Even the demons believe and shudder. (2:14–19)

> Come now, you rich people, weep and wail for the miseries that
> are coming to you. Your riches have rotted, and your clothes are
> moth-eaten. Your gold and silver have rusted, and their rust will
> be evidence against you, and it will eat your flesh like fire. You
> have laid up treasure for the last days. Listen! The wages of the
> laborers who mowed your fields, which you kept back by fraud,
> cry out, and the cries of the harvesters have reached the ears of
> the Lord of hosts. You have lived on the earth in luxury and in
> pleasure; you have fattened your hearts in a day of slaughter. You

have condemned and murdered the righteous one, who does not resist you. (5:1–6)

These are powerful and challenging words that we are not often encouraged to read. Yet they align with what we have come to expect from our scriptural survey so far. Our resources carry obligations to tend to those who are poor or otherwise on the margins in our society. We are reminded that wealth breeds arrogance and blindness to those who are poor. When we are rich we can see the poor as a threat to our belongings rather than as persons created in the image of God to whom we are called to be servants. Perhaps the most frightful reminder in this epistle is the recognition that if belief alone (i.e., belief in certain truth claims) puts one right with God, the demons themselves would be in exemplary shape (2:9).

Colossians 1–2

The first two chapters of the epistle to the Colossians have often been overlooked, but they contain important references to how Christians are to understand God's intentions for public institutions and policies. I will only mention them briefly here as they receive further attention later.

In Colossians 1:15–16, we are told that Christ was the firstborn of all creation and that all "thrones or dominions or rulers or powers" were created "through him and for him." Because governing structures are intended to serve God's expectations, Christians should be concerned that these powers are faithful to that intention. At the very least, this includes structuring our shared life in ways consistent with the themes we have examined so far.

In 2:15, we are told that when Jesus died on the cross he "disarmed" (other, and better, translations say "laid bare" or "unmasked") the "powers." The very powers that were created to serve the divine intent had been corrupted. The fact that they killed the Son of God showed that they had become demonic and now worked against God rather than serving God's intentions. Christians are obliged to speak prophetically to the powers, calling them back to their proper role.

Sabbath

There is one more concept that requires attention before we draw conclusions from the biblical material addressed in this chapter—namely, the topic of "sabbath" or "rest." This topic is rarely addressed in discussions relating to matters of social justice. However, there is very strong reason to believe that it would be a serious oversight to ignore the issue of rest when we are considering the life that pleases God. Here we will consider just a few biblical passages on Sabbath and then we will put them in the context of contemporary life.

We have repeatedly pointed out that God's expectations for us are derived from his own nature or from the example he sets for us. On the subject of Sabbath and rest, consider the creation account of Genesis 2:2: "And on the seventh day God finished the work that he had done, and he rested on the seventh day from all the work that he had done."

There seems to be a certain rhythm to the life God intends for us, one in which regular rest plays an important role. When we get to the Ten Commandments, one of them deals explicitly with honoring the Sabbath and "keeping it holy." The widespread application intended for the Sabbath is evident in Exodus 20:10: "But the seventh day is a sabbath to the Lord your God; you shall not do any work—you, your son or your daughter, your male or female slave, your livestock, or the alien resident in your towns."

As our creator, God knows that regular periods of rest are essential to human flourishing. He commands regular rest out of concern for his creation. We could examine numerous passages from the Hebrew Scriptures that would emphasize this point, but we will leave those for the reader's inquiry.

By the time of the New Testament, Sabbath observance had become highly ritualized and was often observed legalistically. It included a great many rules that identified fairly precisely what could and what could not be done on the Sabbath. Undoubtedly, this was because Sabbath observance had become about obeying a command of God without adequate attention to the underlying question of why Sabbath observance was commanded in the first place. Jesus raised that very question by healing on the Sabbath. When challenged by the Pharisees, Jesus pointed out that God commanded the Sabbath for the benefit of humanity rather than as an abstract command to be obeyed. Thus, doing good on the Sabbath could be consistent with taking the Sabbath seriously. According to Mark 2:27, "Then he said to them, 'The sabbath was made for humankind, and not humankind for the Sabbath.'"

In our contemporary culture, especially in the United States, we have allowed the need for maximizing profits and productivity to drive us toward less and less leisure time. The consequence has been higher levels of stress and stress-related illnesses. When one compares U.S. workers to workers in other countries, it is clear that something is amiss and that human flourishing is not being served. Of course, the causes vary—sometimes companies simply expect too much from employees, but employees can also immerse themselves in lifestyles that lead them to take too little time away for rest. While we need not be strict legalists about Sabbath observance, a proper attitude toward rest is essential to human health and flourishing. In the words of Patrick Miller,

The sabbatical principle says no to the relentless movement of events that seems unchangeable; no to the assumption that, once circumstances have led a person into bondage or slavery, there is no release and the chain of cause and effect must keep going on; no to the economic system that ties people inexorably in debt; no to the claim that the land belongs completely and forever to those who acquire it; and no to the relentless cycle of poverty that is accepted easily as a fact of life. Every seven days, every seven years, every fiftieth year, time that has brought bondage, weariness, debt, poverty, and landlessness is to stop.[7]

Conclusions

This list of biblical passages is hardly exhaustive, but it is representative of what one would find in a more extensive search. From it we can begin to develop a picture of what a public or community life that pleases God would look like. Let us first summarize the various points we have discovered in our examination of Scripture.

1. Because God has entrusted care of creation to humanity, God intends to manage his creation through his human agents. In a sense, God has empowered and authorized humanity to serve as his regents in the world. We must not lose sight, however, of the fact that God intends his creation to be managed in a particular way, namely, in accord with the sorts of expectations we have seen along the way in our study.

2. To say that God has entrusted humanity to manage creation for him is to say that humanity is to serve as creation's stewards or caretakers. As such, humanity is accountable to God for their faithfulness in administering the creation in a manner consistent with God's own intentions. We do not get to do whatever we wish, and we are accountable to God for how we steward his world.

3. One of God's most basic expectations for humanity is that humans be imitators of God. The commands God gives are fre-

quently related to some aspect of God's own nature. We are thus called to imitate God in his care for his creation and for his children. A quick review of chapter 3 will remind us of the primary ways in which we are to be imitators of God.

4. We are to live in ways that embody self-giving love. No one, not even our enemies, is exempt from being loved in this way. In short, we are to consider the interests of others more important than our own interests. This is to be embodied at all levels of our lives, private and public. As we structure our shared lives, we must seek to encourage this way of being. Of course, prioritizing the interests of others is often inconsistent with our normal way of being. Nevertheless, it is clear that God expects it of us.

5. God blesses us in order that we might bless others. This means that we are accountable to God for how we use the blessings given to us and that we are not to use our material or spiritual blessings merely for our own pleasure. God is particularly attentive to how individuals and societies live out this "blessed to be a blessing" way of being, especially with respect to those on the margins of society. Whatever policies and institutions we embrace, this concern cannot be overlooked.

6. God takes seriously the obligation to use our resources for the benefit of others. In many places in Scripture, God's judgment upon humanity is directly related to the failure to be faithful to this use of our resources, whether corporately (Sodom) or personally (Matthew 25).

7. Governments are ordained by God. While God does not indicate that any one particular form of government is to be implemented, Scripture does lead us to conclude that government in general is intended by God as one of the "powers" that orders shared human life. Broadly speaking, God intends governments to serve and empower what might be considered a kingdom agenda.

8. God's justice is very different from what humans often associate with the term "justice." God's justice does not stand over against his mercy or grace. Instead, divine justice unites these concepts so that justice is not merely getting what one deserves but rather includes receiving grace and mercy. We are to embody a sort of justice that blesses without regard to merit and does not characterize the poor as "undeserving."

9. It has been said that a society can be judged by how well it cares for its most marginal members. God himself embodies a particular care for those who are poor or otherwise on the margins of our societies. As people called to imitate God, we must embody this concern as well. This is not merely a personal obligation but a political and public obligation as well.

10. God intends for human economies to be structured so that there will be no poor. God intends for everyone to have "enough" (ready access to life's necessities) and for no one to have an overabundance. At the same time, this does not mean that God expects everyone to have exactly the same. However, there is a big difference between everyone having exactly the same and the large disparities of wealth we see both in the United States and in other parts of the world today. While we tend to dislike the notion of a redistribution of wealth, God does not seem to share that concern. Rather, he is more concerned that we not allow our policies to result in the unjust distribution of wealth.[8]

11. While salvation comes by faith, good works are relevant to human salvation as well. As God brings people into right relationship with himself, he intends that they be purged of greed, selfishness, hard-heartedness, and other sins that prevent us from embodying God's intentions. Societies should be structured in ways that encourage and empower good works. One might object that we should not seek to embody Christian ideals in a religiously pluralistic culture. While I think there are good reasons

to disagree with this objection, perhaps we could agree to begin with the concerns that the different religions do share. If so, we might find that many of them share precisely the concerns that have been raised here.

12. God intends for human life to be structured in such a way that proper opportunities for genuine rest are built into our societies. A regular though not legalistic rhythm of work, rest, and play is required for humans to flourish. Individuals should not run themselves into the ground nor should we conduct ourselves in ways that encourage others to exhaust themselves. To God, human flourishing and the maximization of productivity and profit are hardly the same thing.

It should come as no surprise that there is a remarkable degree of congruence between the findings of chapter 2 and this chapter. We should expect a great deal of similarity between an examination of God's nature and the implications for human life, and an examination of Scripture to determine the kind of shared life that pleases God. And this is exactly what we find. The form of shared human life that pleases God is what flows from having been created in God's image and from attempting to be faithful imitators of God. One could, for example, take each of these points and relate them back to the concluding points of the last chapter.

By now, we are beginning to get a picture of how God expects for us to live together—the priorities he intends us to embody, the manner in which we are to care for each other, and the extent to which our resources carry obligations. We are nearly ready to consider the sorts of public policies and institutions that would serve to encourage the way of life characterized by the conclusions of the last two chapters. Before we do so, two additional issues remain. First, many will read the last two chapters and agree that these are the kinds of things that God expects of us, but they will insist that these expectations apply only to our personal lives rather than public policies and institutions. We need to explore this challenge. Second, we Americans live in an intentionally pluralistic culture, and a guiding principle of our system of government is the separation of church and state. How might Christians both respect this principle and seek to have governments serve a kingdom agenda? To these two questions we now turn our attention.

5

Human Governance
and the Kingdom Agenda

I remember a conversation with Jim Wallis in which he re-
ported discussions with politicians who tended to be un-
sympathetic to attempts to improve the plight of the poor
through legislation. Wallis loved to point out to them the number
of biblical passages that mention the poor or those otherwise on
the margins of society. Initially, these politicians tended to argue
that God was more concerned with saving souls than feeding
mouths. The sheer volume of passages expressing God's concern
for the poor, however, made that a very difficult position to sus-
tain. Over time, those less sympathetic to Wallis's argument for
policy solutions to poverty shifted their positions to argue that
even though God might have a particular concern for the poor,
individuals rather than governments were the solution. These
politicians (amateur theologians) loved to observe that Jesus didn't
say that governments should be the agencies that feed the poor.

Of course, Jesus did not say that explicitly. But there are many things Jesus did not say explicitly. The question is not "Did Jesus say that governments are responsible for the poor?" but rather "Does it follow from Scripture that governments have a role to play in creating and sustaining social justice?" As we shall see, we arrive at a different position if we frame the question this way.

I also had the good fortune of discussing the relationship between Christian faith and politics with a popular conservative blogger whose writings often refer to his Christian faith. "Jesus said that his kingdom was not of this world," this person said to me at one point in our conversation. The arguments tended to defend what might be classified as classical Lockean liberalism, according to which religion is a private matter and arguments on public policy are to be advanced based upon public reasoning and other, more pragmatic, bases. While it is impossible, so the argument goes, that our most basic commitments (religious or not) can be entirely separated from our debates on public policy, the arguments we put forward to defend particular policy positions are not to be made on religious grounds. The liberal democracy that flows from the political theology of Locke essentially seeks to remove the conflicts that have historically tended to rise between those with different religious commitments by removing religion from our public debates. When I asked, "So what should we theologians do? Get out of politics?" it was no surprise that he smiled and said, "Pretty much." When Jesus indicated that his kingdom was not of this world, I am not inclined to think that he meant to affirm what we know as Lockean liberalism or the conclusions that follow from it.

The positions that Wallis encounters and that were defended by my discussion partner are not uncommon in Christian circles. It is certainly true that liberal democracy is the underlying form of our system of government, and the issues suggested by the positions outlined above are important for Christians to work their way through on the way to the public square to engage in political debate. There are four closely related sets of questions that we will consider in this chapter. All are interrelated. First, we must address the question of why, given the personal nature of many of Jesus's teachings, we should think that an understanding of God's intentions for humanity would drive us to political engagement. To be more specific, is it not the church's job to save souls and thus to leave the business of statecraft to political experts? Second, given that the form of government that prevails in the United States is liberal democracy, what is the proper role of Christian faith in our development of public policies? Must Christians bring their policy arguments to the public square and couch them in nonreligious terms? Or can religious arguments be used to defend particular public positions? And how does this relate to developing and embodying a way of being that appropriately respects those of other religious traditions? Third, given a richer, more active view of participation in the political process, can we identify common errors that Christians make as they attempt to participate? If so, what are they, and how might they be overcome? Finally, what are the respective roles for civil government and the church? Again, some argue that Christians ought not to participate in government but rather trust that the reformation of society will be more effectively pursued by grassroots evangelism. Others would simply embrace a sectarianism that leaves the world's problems to the world while Christians focus on the life of the church and its mission. In short, this would lead us to ask whether anything more than a cursory participation in governmental politics is justifiable for Christians.

Once these investigations are complete, we will move to the final chapter, where we will finally take a look at the sorts of public policies and institutions that might serve a kingdom agenda.

For now, let us turn our attention to the four sets of questions identified above, beginning with the first one. Given the personal focus of the message of Jesus, why should Christians try to change public policies and institutions in order to realize a particular vision of a kingdom agenda?

Using care for the poor and those otherwise on the margins of our societies as an example, one version of our first question is whether poverty is a problem to be grappled with by Christians through their local churches, through personal giving and other aid, or a problem that should be undertaken through legislative action. I believe that from a Christian perspective, the answer to both of these questions is yes. First, there can be no question that God intends us as individuals to embody his commands to care for the poor, the widow, and the orphan in our daily lives. The picture we have seen in the discussions so far, and in the various portions of Scripture cited, clearly shows that God intends for us (as individuals and as subcommunities of, say, local churches) to feed the hungry, clothe the naked, give drink to the thirsty, and so forth. We are all to engage in works of mercy that extend care to those in need.

Further, no amount of public or governmental engagement in these concerns can abrogate the obligations that we have personally toward those in need. In other words, the old claim that "I care for the poor by paying my taxes" is never an adequate Christian response. The more immediate concern, however, is those who move from the affirmation of personal responsibility to care for the needy to conclude that, therefore, governments are not enjoined to share this responsibility. Does God exclude social justice from those responsibilities he intends for government?

Drawing on the various biblical passages that were discussed in the last chapter, I argued that God has ordained the existence of governmental institutions. Consider, for example, Genesis 1. There God enjoins humans to exercise stewardship over the world that God had just created. We have argued that the exercise of dominion is to be embodied in a way that reflects our accountability to God as stewards of his good creation. Whatever one thinks about how this "dominion" is to be structured, it seems clear that government has a role to play. Given the competing interests and judgments about what constitutes good stewardship, public policy (and, hence, government) will necessarily be involved.

Second, many of the passages we considered were direct injunctions about requirements that God intended to be included in the law of the people to whom he was speaking. For example, the Years of Jubilee, Years of Release, and collateral laws were not laws that God intended to apply only at some voluntary level relating to interpersonal relationships. Instead, these were to become the law of the land. Some argue that the form of government at the time these laws were given was a theocracy, and therefore we cannot carry these commands directly into our own governmental forms, such as the participatory democracy of the United States in the early twenty-first century. Granting the different forms of government between then and now, even if one recognizes that you cannot directly apply these laws to our own contemporary circumstances, it does not follow that these commands are irrelevant for our own public policies and institutions. There is no reason to think that God's instructions regarding our shared life are somehow different based on the form of government. The form of our engagement might change and the ways in which specific outcomes are accomplished might also change, but not the intended outcomes themselves.

As we saw above, it is God's intention that humans act as his regents, exercising stewardship and care over the creation. It is also God's intention that this stewardship be embodied in ways consistent with the vision of shared human life that we have uncovered in our examination of Scripture. Further, we have seen that the ordination of governmental systems is explicitly affirmed in Romans 13. (Of course, we have also argued that one must consider all of Romans 13, while not separating chapter 13 from the vision of life laid out in Romans 12.) We examined 13:1–7 in our earlier discussion. The first verse of that passage says, "Let every person be subject to the governing authorities; for there is no authority except from God, and those authorities that exist have been instituted by God." The ordination of ruling institutions, aimed to serve the divine intent, is a common theme within Scripture.

As indicated in the preceding chapter, another passage of particular importance is Colossians 1:15–17. Here we are told that all thrones, rulers, powers, and authorities were created by Christ and for Christ. Once again we see that God has created all of the powers for the purpose of serving his long-term, creative purposes. The question is not *whether* God intends governments to have a role in realizing his intentions but rather *what form* this involvement should take.

God's goals for government are outcome related. That is, the particular form does not matter as much as the outcomes. Specifically, they are to encourage communities built around the elevation of the needs of the least of these. Notice, however, that this passage goes beyond simply *ordaining* the "powers." It goes on to affirm that these ruling structures were also created *for* him. The ruling powers, in whatever form they take, are to serve God's intentions. When the powers fail to serve such an agenda, they become demonic and serve to be destructive of the very things they were created to serve. As we noted previously, it would be remarkably strange to think that God has ordained ruling authorities to serve his purpose but then claim that the sorts of things Scripture shows that God cares most about (the marginalized) could be exempted from government involvement. In fact, I would go so far as to argue, based on God's intention that governments serve his agenda, that governments that fail to make the creation of just societies ("just" in the biblical sense) have become demonic and stand in need of prophetic challenge.

Finally, we must be cautious to avoid understanding the biblical affirmation that "Jesus is Lord" too narrowly. This is not merely an affirmation about a Christian's own personal piety, about their own private calling to be obedient to the example of Christ, but rather an affirmation about the entire cosmos. Ultimately, all "thrones, powers, rulers, and authorities" are under the lordship of Christ, and as such they are all to serve the sort of agenda we have already discerned in these pages. When Christians say, on the one hand, "Jesus is Lord," and on the other that governments should not be involved in the realization of a kingdom agenda, they stand in profound contradiction.

Does the objection stand that God intends the poor to be served by individuals but not governments? No. Let me make this point yet once more: it would be bizarre indeed to say that God has ordained the ruling powers to serve his intentions but excludes them from one of the things in Scripture he seems most frequently to express concern about: care for the least of these. We can no more exclude government from a role in this part of a kingdom agenda than we can exclude the responsibilities of individuals. Both individuals and institutions can easily become demonic, selfish, and callous, and we must be ever vigilant to minimize the corruption of the good things God has created.

What sorts of legislative concerns, then, might Christians expect to be embodied in governments that serve the kingdom? Consider the following possibilities:

1. Legislative proposals and outcomes would be tested against the common good and how well they provide for those most at risk in our societies.
2. Governmental authority would be deployed so as to encourage and nurture the sense of self-giving love that we discussed in previous chapters. It would resist the "you are all on your own" mentality and replace it with the "we are all in this together" theme of mutual interdependence.
3. Christians should seek to encourage and reward ways of being that help us to elevate the needs of others over our own. This would have implications, for example, in how we are welcoming the stranger in our land, a particular concern of God's.
4. The potential for Christian involvement ranges across a broad set of issues, including but not limited to economic justice, poverty, environmental concerns, racism, families and communities, and care for the "least of these," wherever they may be found.

This list is not intended to be exhaustive but rather suggestive of the specific ways in which Christians need to measure and judge their involvement in good legislation. Of course, the details of specific policies and institutions will vary based upon particular circumstances.

Jesus and Politics

As noted in the introduction, some people observe that Jesus never explicitly said that governments are the ones primarily responsible for, say, feeding the poor. But there are many situations in contemporary society about which Jesus never spoke explicitly. This common argument from silence really does not help us very much either way and, in fact, often distracts from the deeper and more important question: Can we discern enough from Scripture to be able to draw some conclusions about what would constitute a biblical position even when an issue is not named specifically in Scripture? I hope we have shown that we can.

When we hear the term "political," we often associate it with partisan political maneuvering. Hence, the term carries a rather negative connotation. For Christians to develop a proper view of politics and their involvement in the political process, we must recapture the richer notion of politics as community. N. T. Wright observes that it would have been strange for a first-century Jew to have not seen the political implications of Jesus's words and deeds.[1] The unfortunate narrowing of the term to apply only to partisan politics has not served us well. To see the profoundly political implications of what Jesus was about, consider the following observations:

1. Jesus was executed by the Romans as an enemy of the state.
2. While on the cross, the Romans mockingly identified Jesus as "King of the Jews." They seemed to have been clear about the social and political implications of Jesus's ministry.
3. The early church's affirmation that "Jesus is Lord" was seen as a claim that was political in nature—so much so that the emperor could not tolerate it, and in the days of the early church, confessing Jesus as Lord could cost one his or her life.
4. In the mission statement of Jesus in Luke 4, we see a continuation of the Old Testament prophetic tradition, which often involved calling leaders back to accountability.

In sum, while it is completely correct to say that Jesus avoided *partisan* politics (resisting those who sought to draw him into the

Zealot movement, for example), it is too simplistic to conclude that Jesus's message did not carry serious political implications. Until we come to understand these implications, our public engagement will be either impoverished or nonexistent.

To those who argue that Jesus did not directly engage the first century political powers, we might add to the previous points the differences between the forms of government then and now. The significant differences between living in today's participatory democracy in the United States and living in the early Roman Empire carry some important implications for the manner in which Jesus might have engaged many of these issues. There were no ready means for the common person to participate in the ruling systems in the Roman period. Jesus did not have the options of democratic participation that we do today. Accordingly, any argument that defends either quietism or sectarian withdrawal will require a far more sophisticated defense than merely noting that Jesus did not "participate" in the first century political process. Further, John Howard Yoder has established in his classic *The Politics of Jesus* that the attempt to dismiss Jesus as apolitical simply cannot stand. When the primary means of engagement for those desiring change was armed revolution, Jesus resisted, even though there were strong political implications to what he taught. There is no reason, however, to conclude that such a response applies to all government forms.

For these reasons, I think the argument that God's care for the poor and marginalized is to be only administered through persons in their private roles is mistaken. This position does not properly understand God's concern for the poor, and it fails to account adequately for the extent to which that care is served or hindered by public policies and institutions. Further, our priorities as communities are not only embodied in our personal interactions. What we are most firmly committed to is also made manifest in the sorts of formal mechanisms and structures we put in place in our organized public life.

Regarding the second set of questions, if Christians are to advocate for certain types of policies and institutions, how do we argue about such matters? What counts as evidence in public debate? In the United States, we live in a pluralist culture where policy debates are engaged in by people with a wide range of religious commitments. The founding fathers exhibited a very strong resistance to allowing any one religion to become the state religion. Consequently, it is often argued that debates about public policies and institutions have to be carried out on the basis of a shared commitment to reason as the common ground from which to argue for our positions.

To see the force of such a claim, one only need try to identify other grounds that Christians might use to secure their positions. Shall we say to our non-Christian discussion partners that they should adopt our position because we can give a biblical prooftext for it? Whether our non-Christian interlocutor is a theist or an atheist, it should be obvious that if they do not take the Bible to be normative then they are not likely to be persuaded by biblical arguments. In convincing other Christians, of course, things are quite different (though given the variety of forms of Christian faith, we often have difficulty here as well). However, we have no guarantees that our discussion partners in public debate will be Christian. Should Christians seek to formulate their positions based on some sense of a common rationality in order to be persuasive to non-Christians? Is this a fair expectation, or does it require Christians to abandon basic faith commitments that are simply too important to negotiate?

I believe that Christians should be involved in the political process. Further, as those who believe in the authority of Scripture, we should believe that humanity will be better served as public institutions are brought into conformity with scriptural ideas. This seems to put the basic commitment to the authority of Scripture squarely in opposition to the alleged rule that public debate cannot be based upon scriptural teaching. Is there a way to bridge this gap? I believe there is, and to see it, we will have to return to our earlier discussions about God's intentions and human flourishing.

Let us consider a sample case in which a particular Christian or group of Christians comes to the conclusion that the Bible teaches that a particular way of being is an expression of God's intentions. They have accepted that they cannot simply make their argument to non-Christians on biblical grounds. They might make their argument as follows. First, as we have noted, God does not give us arbitrary commands; rather, he gives commands in order to serve a particular end. That end, in the case of his human creatures, is that they should flourish—not just some of his creatures, but rather all of them. When we speak of creating a society that desires to see all flourish, we are pursuing the *common good*. When we Christians have studied and have come to some conclusions about the life that pleases God, we should argue with confidence that our conclusions serve human flourishing and, accordingly, serve the common good.

Even in a pluralistic culture, because of our confidence as Christians that God's intention for communal life is that all should flourish, we can translate our biblical arguments into arguments for the long-term common good. The form and content of any governmental system for which Christians should argue, then, should be framed as serving the common good of human flourishing. Of course, we have in mind here a very robust sense of the common good, not a shallow version that translates into little more than hedonism, or one that focuses on short-term flourishing at the expense of the long term. Christians can draw their arguments from their faith commitments (as may any other religious person) with the confidence that these can be cast in public debate in terms of the common good. When discussing among ourselves, of course, we Christians should be quite happy to ground our arguments more openly and deeply in Scripture and in the teachings of the Christian tradition.

As long as we take it that God's instructions to us are based on his desire to see long-term human flourishing, then taking the arguments we derive from Scripture and translating them into arguments intending to serve the common good is a perfectly acceptable way to proceed. Of course, there will be debate about what constitutes the common good and, even more so, arguments about how the common good is to be accomplished. Our confidence that God desires our long-term flourishing will enable us to test different policy ideas. We can be confident that correspondence to God's calling to us (caring for those on the margins) will be the path most likely to lead to the outcomes we desire (that there would be no poor among us). However, we cannot underestimate human selfishness and its tendency to tilt the system to our own benefit. Likewise, since we need to be focused on outcomes, we can be quite flexible on the precise policy and institutional means of accomplishing those goals. When we commit to particular policy solutions—whether progressive or conservative, capitalist or socialist—we run the serious risk of losing sight of the higher-level objectives. We Christians should use our faith commitments to help us determine what long-term human flourishing looks like. We should then translate that into language about the common good and argue in the public square on that basis. Finally, we should focus on outcomes and be fairly flexible on specific policies and institutions—as long as they accomplish the identified goals.

Avoiding the Common Errors

The third set of questions relates to the manner in which Christians tend to engage the political process and the common mistakes we make. Are there common, identifiable mistakes that Christians often make in the manner in which they participate in political debate? If so, what improvements can be made? I think there are three common mistakes. First, we tend to put too much trust in the political process for making the world a better place. From what has preceded, it is obvious that I think that the public policies and institutions can serve a kingdom agenda. The concern I express here relates to putting *too much* confidence in them. Second, there is a common tendency to be overly narrow in determining what counts as a moral issue. For those with a more robust grasp of Jesus's teachings and the teachings of Scripture overall, this creates the impression that we have narrowed the moral agenda in a way that serves partisan interests. Finally, and closely related to the second point, not only do we tend to be overly narrow in deciding what counts as a moral issue but we also often get the priorities backwards or otherwise out of alignment with the teachings of Scripture.

Keeping the right balance between a proper set of expectations for the manner in which public policies and institutions can serve a kingdom agenda on the one hand and putting too much trust in them on the other hand is often difficult. I recall a particular seminary professor who frequently mourned the extent to which Christians trusted the legislative process rather than sound church teaching to help create a "moral" society. If only we could get the right set of laws in place, so the argument he resisted tended to go, then we could create a more biblical world (or country, at least). He did not suggest that trusting in legislation was never appropriate but rather that this aspect had become overemphasized to the point that some Christians seemed to have lost sight of the church and its responsibilities altogether. Christians must not forget the fact that, at the end of the day, our trust is in God and in his church, not in any political process or form.

The choice is not between either complete trust in political institutions and mechanisms or no trust in them at all. Rather, the issue is how to rightly balance the trust, and therefore the degree of time, one invests in each. This becomes somewhat more complex when we recognize that God calls different people to different vocations. Not all will be called to focus on governmental politics, but God will call some to this level of involvement as their Christian vocation. For most Christians, we ought to expect that our primary service to the kingdom will be directed through the church. And we should encourage and prayerfully support each other regardless of our respective vocational callings.

That said, there are two additional common errors that we Christians make, and in a sense, they are simply different versions of putting too much trust in the political process. The first one arises when we begin to see policy changes as the solution to humanity's ills apart from the need to bring people into right relationship with God. This error becomes most evident when the vast majority of our conversation revolves around reforming political and legislative structures rather than the reformation of the church or the transformation of persons. It would be a marvelous thing to see the elimination of poverty in our time. However, if the elimination of poverty is accomplished apart from faith and relationship to God, have we solved the problem of feeding bellies while leaving people starving spiritually? William Cavanaugh makes this point in his book *Theopolitical Imagination* when he notes our tendency to buy into the modern nation-state so deeply that it becomes a competitive and alternative soteriology to that offered by God through his church.[2] Human flourishing involves both physical and spiritual flourishing.

In the end, to make this error is to succumb to idolatry, that is, to place our ultimate hope in something other than God. Ideally, proper balance on these matters is best maintained when political engagement is rooted in the church rather than apart from it. Christians on both the political right and the political left fall prey to this temptation. Changing societies through the moral engagement of culture by the church is a long and difficult process. One can understand the lure of easy change that might come through simply changing legislation, but we as Christians dare not fall prey to it. And the alternative is not sectarian withdrawal—that would be to replace one error with another. Keeping proper balance is essential.

The second error, though thankfully not quite as prevalent, comes in the form of an explicit desire to make the United States into a theocracy. There are those whose stated goal is to bring the nation under "biblical rule." This is often taken to mean full observation of the laws in the Old Testament, including stoning adulterers and the like (though, strangely, there has been little mention of such things as the Years of Release and Years of Jubilee). But apart from some very bad and anachronistic readings of the Hebrew Bible, there is no biblical basis for attempting to create a theocracy. Neither a theocratic rule of the political left nor of the political right would open the space God intends. Theocracy is a form of idolatry that puts ultimate trust in political institutions rather than in the Spirit speaking through the church. In an odd way it seeks to meld church and state into a monolithic structure. Historically speaking, attempts to unite Christian faith with governing institutions have been disasters, as have attempts to completely separate governance from religious faith. We should not attempt to re-create the error of theocracy but rather let the church (and other religious traditions) offer competent and nonpartisan moral critique of governing institutions.

Complexities abound here. If God has granted us free will, one could rightly ask whether one can "legislate morality" in the first place (though of course we certainly do legislate "moral behaviors"). Where does God intend the coercive power of the state to be deployed? There must be a balance between legislation and personal freedoms. In light of the biblical weight given to serving the common good, we should be inclined to grant freedom in personal matters that have minimal impact on the common good.[3] However, in areas where our positions impact the ability of all to flourish, Christians should be on the front line calling for laws that serve the common good (and therefore ultimately a kingdom agenda). A firm commitment to the common good, and the related idea of social justice, does not require that we think that, say, economic justice can only be satisfied if all persons have the same income. The term "justice" is big enough to allow differences based on a number of factors. The Scriptures recognize different levels of wealth, but we must not lose sight of two important points: (1) those who have much should not have too much, and those who have little should not have too little; and (2) God's gifts should always be seen as gifts given for us to bless others. In the next chapter, we will consider other areas where framing our arguments in terms of the common good might require the "right to sin" (or even "the right to heresy"[4]) with regard to certain kinds of personal behavior.[5]

We have already wandered into the second and third problems, namely, the narrow manner in which moral issues tend to be defined and the priorities that are assigned to moral issues. Because these issues are so closely related, we will examine them concurrently, though we need not expand too much beyond what we have already commented. People both on the political left and the political right have a tendency to narrow the sorts of things that they consider to be morally significant. This can be captured most broadly by observing that the political right has a tendency to see "personal" rather than "institutional" sin. The political left tends to err in the other direction. Unfortunately, nonreligious people clearly see the hypocrisy of this. Those on the right, for example, talk about taking Scripture seriously and following Jesus, but then they focus on issues Jesus never addressed or that get only secondary attention in the overarching biblical narrative. Those on the left too often engage in a facile "red letter" Christianity that focuses on Jesus's words but is largely unaware of the context in which those words appear in the biblical narratives.[6]

Without a broad-based agenda that brings together the Old and New Testaments, Christians on the right and on the left will continue to pursue narrow and improperly prioritized agendas. We will save our examination of policies and institutions that would serve a kingdom agenda for the next chapter. For now, let us note that a common error Christians make in political engagement, whether from the political left or the political right, is that they too easily reduce the complex array of moral expectations God has for us. By doing so, both sides betray crucial aspects of what it means to be followers of Jesus.

Church and Government

This brings us to the fourth and final set of questions, which might be summarized by the following question: Given that the hope of the world is in God's work through Jesus and his church, how shall we understand the relative roles of the church and governmental systems?

We have argued extensively that a sectarian withdrawal from participation in government is problematic for a number of reasons. We have also resisted putting too much confidence in governments to solve all the ills of humankind. To follow that path is to end up in an idolatry of the right or an idolatry of the left. A third inadequate position that we have not yet critiqued is the tendency to divide the world into a "political realm" and a "spiritual realm," where the former is ruled by appropriate governmental systems and the latter is ruled by the church. Consider, Jesus's statement in John 18:36: "Jesus answered, 'My kingdom is not from this world. If my kingdom were from this world, my followers would be fighting to keep me from being handed over to the Jews. But as it is, my kingdom is not from here.'"

The claim often made from this passage is that Jesus is denying a role in the governmental systems of this world. However, as we discussed earlier, a better way of understanding this is to see that Jesus is denying that his kingdom *has its origins* in this world. It is not a "worldly kingdom" in that sense. Rather, Jesus's kingdom is radical, and Jesus establishes his lordship over all of the universe—including our existing governmental systems. As such, they are finally or ultimately accountable to him, as are we.

From a Christian perspective, the fact of the matter is wrapped up in the rich affirmation that "Jesus is Lord." While there might be some sense in which the church is steward of the spiritual realm and appropriate governmental systems are stewards of the political realm, the most important affirmation from a Christian perspective is that both are empowered by and accountable to their Lord Jesus. Once again we conclude that Christian participation in the prevailing political forms is both appropriate and salutary within the bounds of one's own personal vocational calling and within the bounds described here.

There is, however, a right and reasonable division of labor between church on the one hand and public policies and institutions on the other. This is the grain of truth to be found in the tendency to divide these into different spheres of responsibility. It is not a division that puts one over against the other but rather one that allows the two to complement each other. It is not wise, for example, to entrust governments with the responsibility to establish the appropriate forms of worship conducted by different religious groups. (The one exception to this would be a form of worship that harmed the common good—one would not expect governments to remain disinterested, for example, while a particular religion practiced human sacrifice.) Similarly, we would not expect that churches would do a particularly good job of directly managing public transportation, police forces, or international policy. Christians do have things to say about serving the common good. Government employees (who, in a democratic form of governance, are ultimately *our* employees) ought to be hired first and foremost on their ability to effectively accomplish the ends assigned by various policies and legislation. Church staff ought to be hired based on their ability to administer the affairs of the church and its worship. As simple as the principle is, it is surprising how often one hears arguments, for example, that a particular candidate should be supported *just because* they happen to be a Christian.

Stanley Hauerwas has observed that the most basic job of the church is just to be the church—to embody a different way of being that arises from following the radical Rabbi from Nazareth who managed to get himself executed on a cross outside the city walls.[7] The twin temptations to either shortcut the process by too heavily relying on legislation or to withdraw into sectarianism should not be underestimated. Maintaining a position that allows the church primarily to *be the church* while still offering a critique to the political institutions is difficult. It is, however, critical for our best serving a kingdom agenda at all levels of human interaction—public and private. The role of the church is to just be the church, but in so doing the church should both embody and speak critique to the powers that have been corrupted and no longer serve a kingdom agenda.

Conclusions

Scripture recognizes a place for civil and governmental institutions in realizing and ordering the public life that conforms to God's intentions. Further, since we have argued that God intends for all to flourish and that his intentions are consistent with long-term human flourishing, we as Christians should not feel timid about arguing for the biblical image of public life to the extent that it serves the common good. Consequently, we should be encouraged and empowered to argue for laws that ensure, for example, protection from exploitation. There are a variety of ways in which issues might be addressed legislatively, and Christians may choose to support particular legislation or more overarching legislative directions or outcomes. The possibility of both public and private involvement in the solutions should not be overlooked. To the extent possible, the two should proceed hand in hand.

Earlier we suggested that we cannot move directly from Scripture to policy directions. Instead, we must move indirectly. In order to do this, we must both consider particular scriptural examples as well as attempt to discern what God intended by those particular scriptural examples. Recall our discussion of the laws of gleaning, Release, and Jubilee. As the reader may recall, the gleaning laws require those with farms, vineyards, and the like to leave some fruit in the field for the poor to gather for themselves. This combines care for the poor with a means of self-provision. The laws of Release require that debts be forgiven every seventh year, and the laws of Jubilee require that all lands be returned to the ancestral owners every fifty years. In light of our analysis so far, we can draw the following conclusions about these laws:

1. God is concerned that there not be a permanently dispossessed class of those who live on the margins and are particularly vulnerable to exploitation—or worse, left to die.

2. All three of these laws are oriented toward preventing or at least alleviating poverty. Gleaning laws provided a means for the poor to gather food, the laws for Release made sure that individuals did not become permanently trapped in debt (notice that lending is not the problem but rather how lending might lead to exploitation), and the laws of Jubilee aim to prevent the permanent loss of land.

3. These laws imitate the God who cares for those on the margins. By commanding us to do so, God not only provides for the poor but shows concretely what it means to imitate God's character, to be created in God's image.

If we can agree that these are the underlying concerns that God had in mind with the laws we identified, and if we can agree that simply importing these laws into our contemporary situation is not the best solution, we can then ask what sorts of laws Christians might support in order to meet these same objectives. To that goal, and thus the end of our study, we now turn.

6

Public Policy
and the Kingdom Agenda

As we begin our long-promised consideration of public policies that would serve a kingdom agenda, there are a few points that we need to keep in mind. First and perhaps most important, the proposals that I will put on the table over the next few pages are intended to begin discussion more than anything else. As I have argued, serving a kingdom agenda is generally not a matter of commitment to certain policies but rather to a set of policy outcomes. In the preceding chapters, I have presented a series of arguments for what those outcomes should be, relative to such issues as care for the marginalized, just economic systems, and so on. Accordingly, as you read through the different policies, consider ways in which they can be improved, or consider alternative policies that will better serve God's intentions. In addition, because my goal is to open dialogue rather than to win an argument on particular policy positions, I will not take time to develop the positions in detail or to assess them by way of historical analysis. I leave that as an exercise for the reader who wishes to engage the process and either affirm these positions or make counterproposals.

Second, it is important to minimize the impact of our own ideological commitments so that they do not blind us either to the consideration of these proposals or to constructive alternatives to them. We must be driven both by faithfulness to a way of being that flows from our Christian faith (we cannot "cease to be Christian" in order to accomplish some perceived end) while also considering the relevant pragmatic factors. Obviously, the best policies are ones that are consistent with the life of faith, satisfy God's intentions, and actually work. Too often policy ideas are dismissed because they are perceived to run afoul of some particular theoretical concern that we have. Careful assessment and experimentation will be important. We will need to guard against the voices of "experts" that can become little more than apologists for wealthy, powerful interests. We must never underestimate the power of self-interest to pervert our perception of the truth. It is hard to get a person to believe *x* when his paycheck depends on not believing *x*, to paraphrase Upton Sinclair.

Third, it is important to recognize that the only balance to private power is public power. Of course, the reverse is also true. When either public or private power is out of balance, the opportunity for abuse presents itself. Ideally, we will look for solutions that bring together the private and the public sectors in cooperative, win-win scenarios. Unfortunately, this is rarely tried because proponents of various sides have certain theoretical commitments that lead them away from cooperation. We have to overcome this resistance. Our attempt to forge a way of being faithful to God's intent must not be disrupted by those who would presuppose that free markets or governments are always more effective in accomplishing our desired ends. The reality is more complex and subtle, and we will have to be open to having our own favorite solutions critiqued—and possibly proven wrong.

Fourth, another way of making the third point is to say that we need to bring together the best thinking of the political left and the political right in forging solutions to the problems we face. Those on the left will need to be more willing to consider the deployment of free market mechanisms, and those on the right will have to be more willing to see a positive role for the public sector. Rather than each side saying that the other cannot be trusted, we must call forth the "better angels" of each side to draw us into effective cooperation. The current political climate is, frankly, one that renders such cooperation unlikely. With both sides pursuing power for power's sake, often throwing the common good under the bus, we will need strong and prophetic voices that call for a better way. It would be a delight to find people of faith genuinely willing to lead such discussions.

Fifth, it is important to reflect on the significance of the so-called "social contract." This is an abstract way of drawing attention to the fact that all members of a society engage in its construction in order to gain particular benefits. When the social contract becomes skewed, say, by assigning too much value to capital and not enough to labor or vice versa, one side or the other is no longer the beneficiary of the common good. When societies fail to serve the common good and instead serve particular, special interests, we set up a condition that invites the collapse of the social contract that binds us together in peace.[1]

Sixth and most important, we Christians simply can never lose sight of the fact that our ultimate hope is in Christ and his church. Governments and public institutions are ordained by God to serve their particular purpose in a kingdom agenda. As Christians we should insist that governments live up to the divine intent, but in so doing, we should not place our ultimate hope in them. They serve the kingdom, but they do not replace it. Too often, Christians of all stripes seem to put more faith in the nation-state to alleviate problems than is consistent with the call of Christ and his church (though, sometimes, we place too little in it as well). Let us call our governments to serve the divine agenda, but let us not lose sight of the bearer of our final hope. Some writers such as Stanley Hauerwas and William Willimon have identified what they and others have come to call "American civil religion." By this phrase they refer to a version of the faith that closely identifies the American nation-state with the kingdom of God. Though rarely so crass as to openly admit it, those seduced by American civil religion tend to equate the faithful exercise of faith with patriotism and the presuppositions of the nation-state with those of the Christian faith. We must come to see, as we suggested in the last chapter, that this is merely a form of idolatry that must be energetically resisted.

If our discussion so far accurately reflects the sort of public life that pleases God, then it is time to ask what sort of policy positions Christians ought to embrace. In other words, how does a commitment to the biblical view of public life guide decisions about which policies Christians should support? One should not engage this question presupposing that the answer will lie at either pole of the false dichotomy between public and private solutions. Nor should one expect that there is a single answer to the question. Rather, a wide range of possible cooperative engagements between private and public institutions may produce something close to a biblical view. For example, there is widespread agreement that if only the political will existed, serious reduction in child poverty (both domestically and internationally) is quite achievable. We have the technology and we have the wealth to do it. Unfortunately, the debate is often over competing ideologies rather than concrete solutions aimed at bringing together the best of both public and private institutions. What we lack is not the know-how and the resources but rather the political will to make it happen. Likewise, the debate over whether pure market forces or extensive government regulation should determine appropriate wage levels frequently leaves families with too little food on the table. First and foremost, Christians must focus on specific ways in which public and private institutions can be brought into alignment so as to encourage and empower human flourishing at all levels. We should be looking for ways to realize the kinds of things we have discovered in our discussion so far—again, not necessarily through the same means, but for the purpose of accomplishing the ends we have discerned that God intends for us.

Again, both public and private sectors are necessary. For example, during natural disasters, churches are often first in line to give relief to hungry, displaced people. Yet churches are not able to rebuild infrastructure, and the scale of resources needed for restoration frequently far exceeds the reach of charitable efforts. The outpouring of charity subsequent to Hurricane Katrina is probably the single most generous outpouring of charitable giving on record. However, even that overwhelmingly generous response was estimated to be in excess of $50 billion short of what was needed. To deal with problems of this scope and magnitude, we must come to see that both private and public resources are required.

Without suggesting that the following positions are nonnegotiable from a Christian perspective, let us consider a range of possible policy positions and reflect on how they might satisfy the kinds of concerns outlined throughout this book. In each case, I will name a policy position, briefly describe it, and then comment on how it helps realize the divine intent for our shared public life.

Safety Nets

People inevitably find themselves in intractable situations—situations that put them and their families at risk in one way or another. Sometimes we will see a homeless person and refer to them as one who has "fallen on hard times." The question we have to address as Christians is, what obligations do we have to such individuals and families? Scripture is clear that those who are in jeopardy are to be helped back up. The debate often revolves around what form such help is to take.

Let me begin by saying that I am sympathetic to those who say that help for those on the margins ought to come from the church first. However, I have to part company when some take the next step and suggest that such help can *only* come through the church. While we should be happy to see churches taking on ever increasing roles in the alleviation of the suffering of those in crisis, we simply cannot preclude government from being involved in this work. This is particularly true when churches are simply unable or unwilling to take on the enormous task. Human lives are just too precious and important. Poverty rates are too high for government not to be involved.

Consider three examples of programs designed to help those in crisis: unemployment insurance, social welfare programs, and Medicaid. The first is designed to help those in jeopardy from having lost a job; unemployment insurance provides a bridge to the next job. The other two programs provide safety nets for those whose income level will not allow them the security necessary to live. Given our scriptural analysis, it is difficult to see the basis for suggesting that it is consistent with Christian faith to be against government involvement in these areas. This would be to argue that it would be better to allow individuals and families (specifically women and children) to suffer than to allow government intervention. In fact, it is important to note that in order to embody the mutual interdependence that God expects, we should take steps as a society as a whole to ensure strong safety nets for those who fall on unfortunate times. Yes, the church can and should make this a priority as well, but the priorities for meeting the needs of the poorest must also be a part of the national commitments expressed in governmental policy. Again, it is hard to see how the public institutions God ordained to organize our public lives, namely governments, should be exempted from caring for the poor—one of the most frequently expressed concerns in the Bible.

At the end of the day, we should not be driven by ideological commitments that blind us to the needs of those around us or prevent us from testing various strategies and implementing the best ones. Christians should support a strong social safety net based on our examination of the way of being together that pleases God. If and when the church demonstrates its willingness and ability to expand its share of the load for providing societal safety nets, then we may find a decreased need for government programs. But the first priority must be the creation of communities of mutual interdependence wherein all are assured a degree of safety in crisis circumstances.

Progressive Income Tax

"To whom much has been given, much will be required" (Luke 12:48). This text alone would hardly be adequate to justify a progressive income tax. In fact, this passage is not related to the question of taxation at all. However, when it is coupled with the biblical vision that those who have much do not have too much and that those who have little do not have too little (2 Cor. 8:15), one can see how progressive tax policy can serve a number of the goals of Scripture. First, these policies can serve as a way to make sure that the least of these are not left behind. Those on the lowest end of the economic scale often must make difficult choices between, say, food and medicine. Their level of income, if indeed they have an income at all, does not allow them access to basic life needs. A progressive income tax aims to ensure that taxes do not prevent access to these essentials for those who are poorest.

Consider, for example, the working poor who are trying to make ends meet on an income level corresponding to the minimum wage (just over $15,000 per year). This is barely enough to pay for basic needs, much less taxes. Those in higher tax brackets pay taxes out of money that would otherwise pay for luxuries and creature comforts while those in lower tax brackets must pay taxes out of the money they need to cover basic life necessities. To whom much is given, much is required, and vice versa.

Secondly, a progressive income tax also helps to prevent the accumulation of wealth in the hands of a few and, thereby, prevents the continual slanting of the economic playing field ever more in favor of the well-to-do. Many of the laws in Scripture are focused on preventing the creation of an economic system that allows for the concentration of wealth. Such concentration results in numerous social ills. Sadly, too often cynics argue that progressive taxation is really driven by the "politics of envy." It is preeminently the job of Christians to remind people that the issue is not one of envy but rather the biblical injunction to care for those on the margins and, even more, to eradicate unjust social structures that force people onto the margins in the first place.

As we noted in the first item above, societies that are aligned with a kingdom agenda must take seriously the need to fund the safety nets required to tend to those who fall on hard times. A progressive income tax structure makes sure that funding for those safety nets falls to those who are most able to afford it.

As Christians, we must not fail to care for the poor in favor of "personal responsibility" or "tough love." Are there places for personal responsibility and tough love? Of course, but they are not an excuse to stand by and do nothing when our neighbors are in need.

Race Relations

Scripture reminds us that there are no longer distinctions of race, gender, and class (Galatians 3) in the world as God intends it and that God does not respect one person more than another (Acts 10). From this and from all that we have discussed, there can be no doubt that there is no biblical basis for racial discrimination. The model following from the life and teachings of Jesus is that there is now "neither Jew nor Greek." In the immediate context, it is clear that all of God's human creatures possess equal dignity. This is not the same as saying that God blesses each with the exact same set of blessings or talents, only that those blessings and talents are not parceled out on the basis of race, gender, or the like. His love is boundless and overlooks the superficial differences that we too often allow to separate us. Attempts to root racial discrimination in Scripture, as was so common during the era of slavery, are still blights on the history of some traditions of biblical interpretation. Yet it is always easy to criticize the past. While we are now at a point in time when that misuse of Scripture from an earlier period is seen for what it was, we still struggle with hidden (and, sadly, sometimes not so hidden) expressions of racism in our contemporary society.

One of the questions we must take on to understand the roots of racism is what motivates us to feel the need to exclude the "other." I use the term "other" to capture a more robust sense of otherness than, say, simply another person like us, but without necessarily restricting our conversation to racial differences. Most frequently, the reason for discrimination in all its various forms is to exclude "others" from scarce or limited resources. These resources need not be material, but rather can include all the resources that enable us to flourish—food, shelter, security, peace, and so forth.

We humans fear the uncertainties of existence. We fear going hungry, not having enough for our family, and being left out in the cold. In short, we fear inadequate access to the things that enable us and our community to flourish. This creates a tendency to hoard whatever resources we can get our hands on because we believe that this will protect us against those uncertainties. Of course, we hoard resources at someone else's expense. As Hobbes and others have noted, we form societies in order to help us escape selfishness—"a most brutish existence," to use Hobbes's phrase for it.

Since we do not want to exist in a world where it is "everyone for themselves," we form communities and subcommunities that band together to protect our members from "them." Who are "they"? Most likely, we make the "others" the ones who are most different from us—different in race, class, and the like. We then create societal and communal barriers to "them" getting the limited resources that we want for ourselves. Race has been, throughout history, a simple and significant way of determining "us" from "them." Of course, the biblical injunctions to care for our neighbors make it clear that we have no acceptable basis for excluding others. This is particularly evident when we consider that the paradigm for caring for others is loving our enemies.

Recall our discussion of the Good Samaritan. How can we be faithful followers of Jesus and faithful imitators of God when we allow race or other distinctions to be used as means to exclude others from the full bounty of God's blessing? Whatever the final form of government we adopt, it is clear that there can be no moral basis for racial discrimination (or the other kinds of discrimination we have mentioned above). Thus, we must structure our societies in ways that prevent our normal tendencies to divide the world into "us" and "them."

Social Security

Before the enactment of social security legislation, the poverty rate among seniors was near 30 percent. In a report published recently,[2] it was estimated that just over 40 percent of the senior population would have been in poverty in 2009 without the resources provided by social security.[3] While red flags are often raised regarding social security, and while many advocate its privatization, social security has been remarkably successful in lifting the elderly out of poverty. Does that mean that no changes should ever be made to the social security program? Of course not. But it does mean that we must never lose sight of the intent of the program (insurance against the elderly dropping into poverty) and we must make sure that any changes leave that goal intact.

We have reviewed several biblical passages that support the basic idea behind the implementation of the social security program. First, we must keep in mind the various injunctions to care for those on the margins of society. There are few groups more at risk of falling onto the margins than the elderly, and the high poverty rates prior to the inception of social security are adequate evidence of this fact. God's concern for the least of these undoubtedly includes the elderly in our modern cultural climate. Second, the command to "honor your father and your mother" is serious enough for God to include it in the Ten Commandments. How can any culture say it has taken seriously the call to honor our fathers and mothers if it allows a third to a half of them to languish in poverty in their senior years? As Christians we should celebrate the fact that we have policies in place that ensure care for our parents.

There are a host of individual issues that we, as Christians, can be quite flexible about. For example, whether the retirement age should be increased as life expectancy increases can be left to pragmatic concerns as long as the overarching vision is not lost. Would it be acceptable to privatize social security? Perhaps. We must not lose sight of the fact, however, that the basic idea of social security is to ensure a basic level of sustenance for the elderly and to prevent them from falling into poverty. Anything that would put that at risk without also providing protection would be unacceptable. Too often Wall Street money managers see the funds potentially set aside for social security payments as ways to improve their own profitability. Changes to the program must ensure the ongoing security of the funding for our seniors.

Medicare

Just as with social security, Medicare came into existence because access to health care was hard for seniors to come by. One does not have to be wedded to any particular approach to meeting our obligations to the elderly. But returning to a laissez-faire approach that makes accessing care a personal responsibility is simply inadequate from a Christian perspective, especially in a culture that allows insurers to charge exorbitant prices for care.

Minimum Wage Laws

From what we have studied so far, how can we develop a picture of God's expectations for fair employee compensation? First, we should recall that there is no biblical basis for arguing that all persons should be paid the same, regardless of the nature of their work. The straw man often raised against minimum wage laws is that those who favor them are really after equal outcomes. At the same time, to say that Scripture does not require equal outcomes is not to say that Scripture is not concerned about outcomes at all. Scripture is consistently concerned about those most at risk in societies.

In a culture that too often favors capital over labor, we do well to recall that making money from money was eschewed by Scripture and by the church for centuries. We ought to ensure at least a degree of balance in the economic playing field by preventing employee compensation from dropping to exploitative levels. Employers have responsibilities to their workers, not just to their shareholders. Minimum wage laws are one way to ensure that minimum wages do not fall below a certain level, thus preventing the one who has little from having too little.

In most areas of the United States today, estimates place a *living wage* (the income level one actually needs to access the essentials) well above the current minimum wage. The biblical picture of economic justice would hardly be satisfied by conditions that allow the lowest paid employees to work hard but forever remain in poverty. One is reminded of the Tennessee Williams tune about mining tons of coal but getting only "another day older and deeper in debt." The song refers to the perversity of "company towns," which were owned by mining companies. They had cleverly balanced what they paid employees and what they charged them in their company stores so that workers were never quite able to make ends meet. Workers found themselves growing deeper in debt no matter how hard they worked. One wonders how God's judgment will fall on those responsible for such exploitative practices, especially in light of his judgment of the rich man who ignored Lazarus. Those who work and abide by the rules ought to be paid at a level that allows them to live and flourish. Surely, under the biblical vision that none should have too little, one can easily defend legislation that makes this a reality. Wage-related laws provide one of the means to ensure this.

Earned Income Credit/Dependent Child Credit

The last point notwithstanding, there are some circumstances that would make paying a just wage difficult. In such cases, we must recall that Scripture calls us to treat both the poor and the wealthy justly (even if Scripture's sense of what it means to treat someone justly is different from our own general tendencies). How might we balance these concerns? When circumstances make it difficult or impossible for a business to pay a just wage, we must find ways to take that burden upon ourselves. This is precisely what the earned income tax credit does by assuring that "work works" when a just wage is not feasible. Rather than simply excluding those cases from justice, we have developed the earned income tax credit (EITC) as a means of sharing the burden.

Why is this just? It can be argued, for example, that in some sectors lower payrolls benefit the rest of us by keeping labor expenses low. Perhaps lower wages make certain products or services affordable and marketable in the first place. However, if the public at large benefits from what would constitute exploitative wages for some, then the public at large ought to bear the burden of a just wage. Earned income tax credits are a way to embody the sort of mutual interdependence noted above as central to a biblical way of living. These credits enable society as a whole to bear the burden so that economic justice is satisfied. No one should be left on the margins because some people have ideological commitments to free markets or to "personal responsibility." Our ideological commitments must be rooted in God's expectations for what our shared life should look like.

Access to Health Care

It is hard to imagine that God's intentions that all should flourish could be satisfied without health care access. For too many people, quality and length of life are directly connected to whether they have ready access to health insurance. Current estimates of the number of unnecessary deaths resulting from inadequate health care access are as high as 45,000 per year.[4] Why? Most frequently it is because they do not have access to health care insurance. We allow many inequities and inadequacies in our health care system. For example, the very individuals who are too poor to buy health insurance (or who are denied it for other reasons) are the same ones who are charged the highest rates at the doctor. Insurance companies use their bargaining power to purchase services at steep discounts, but when the poor, uninsured person is treated, they end up being charged the highest rates. Over the last few years, during a period of economic recession, many cities have had to reduce or close public clinics that served as a safety net for the poor, leaving even more people with inadequate access to health care.

A variety of other injustices permeate our health care system. "Preexisting conditions" are used as a basis to exclude people from coverage, but they are the ones who most need it. Too often, preventative measures are undercovered by insurance, which encourages people to wait until they are sick to receive medical attention. In the long run, the costs end up being higher. Insurance companies are increasingly imposing onerous co-pays and so-called out-of-pocket payments as ways of transferring costs from insurance companies to the insured. All the while, of course, insurance company profits soar. In an earlier time in America, insurance companies were treated as nonprofits. The belief was that some things were so important for society to flourish that they should not be distracted by the need to make profits. Health care was seen as one of those things. This is no longer the case. The need to drive profits upward has pitted human flourishing against profitability, and sadly, profitability often wins. As I write this book, we are engaged in a debate about health care reform in the United States. Oddly, many Christians—the very folks who, on biblical grounds, should be supporting health care reform—are arrayed against it. The final form of the legislation, if there is to be any, remains unclear.

Health care costs can also contribute to homelessness and poverty. The costs associated with major illnesses frequently force people into bankruptcy and foreclosure. Without comprehensive reform that outlaws a number of the abuses we see under the current system, too many people will fall short of flourishing because we allow our own self-interests or business profitability to trump what should be a clear biblical mandate. The healing of various ailments, regardless of whether their primary manifestation is physical, mental, or spiritual, is a repeated theme in the Bible. God desires human well-being. Ensuring access to health care is one way to imitate this.

Estate and Inheritance Taxes

We have already mentioned that estate and inheritance taxes serve a similar function to the Years of Release and especially the Years of Jubilee from the Old Testament. In our discussions about the Years of Jubilee, we noted that God likely commanded the observance of Years of Jubilee to avoid the development of a permanently dispossessed class of people and the accumulation of vast holdings of wealth in the hands of a few. Rather than allowing a family's bad luck or unfortunate choices to result in chronic poverty for successive generations, Jubilee enacted a periodic leveling of the economic playing field. Rather than allowing those in power to use that power to further slant the playing field in their favor, God's commands to restore the land to its ancestral owners effectively relocated power in the hands of others. While estate and inheritance taxes are often mischaracterized, they can readily serve the same purpose by preventing the consolidation of wealth across generational lines. They can also level the economic playing field and minimize the chances of a permanently dispossessed class of people.

There is nothing inherent in estate and inheritance taxes that makes them the only way to accomplish these ends. For example, the Years of Jubilee are different in form even if similar in intent. Our context is different, so we cannot import this practice directly into our contemporary culture. We must often move indirectly from Scripture to contemporary social structures. There may be other and better means to accomplish these ends than estate and inheritance taxes. However, simple appeals to abolish the taxes without attention to the underlying problem they address is hardly being responsible to a biblical vision of life together. The cynicism of those who label the estate and inheritance taxes a "death tax" must be resisted.

Bankruptcy Laws

For approximately fifteen hundred years, the church refused to allow charging interest in order to make money. Scripture explicitly rejects the practice.[5] While we do not have to apply the Bible directly, we should at least entertain the possibility that lending at interest is problematic. Great care is taken in the Bible to prevent those with money from exploiting others. In addition to the laws against charging interest, God gave restrictive collateral laws (Release and Jubilee), which recognized that bad luck and other circumstances should not be allowed to condemn people to poverty forever. We argued above that estate and inheritance laws are one mechanism for dealing with this. Fair bankruptcy laws are another.

One of the sad realities of life is the perversity in which some financial institutions are willing to engage in order to increase profits—complicated forms that make genuine disclosure a joke, misrepresentations about their own financial stability, and predatory lending practices, just to name a few. Certainly, part of the so-called collapse of the housing bubble of the first decade of the millennium is related to financial institutions seeking out and exploiting people by encouraging them to commit to loans that they ultimately had no hopes of repaying. From a Christian perspective, we can never be satisfied with the old motto *caveat emptor* ("let the buyer beware") as an adequate basis for a just system of exchange. No, we must also be willing to hold accountable those who engage in immoral and deceptive (even if legal!) trade practices that abuse those for whom God expresses most concern. Fair bankruptcy laws must include provisions to hold accountable not only those who invest unwisely but also those who willingly encourage and persuade people to invest unwisely. Fair bankruptcy laws should not excuse someone trying to "game the system," but they also must not overly punish honest mistakes. The old adage, "An ounce of prevention is worth a pound of cure" might well apply here—better to create systems of accountability for those who would encourage unwise investments and loans than to wait for a collapse.

Monopoly Laws

Those who argue for free market forces and for market competition are often also the most unwilling to take on the question of the monopolization of business power. Consider the question of fair pricing. A fair price for a good or service is supposedly whatever a willing, free, and unencumbered purchaser would be willing to pay for it. However, is any purchaser really free and unencumbered when markets are monopolized? The more critical the good or service is, the more urgent the need for it is. Under these conditions, one can imagine sellers charging irrational prices for goods and services. A culture aiming to live together as God intends needs to have strong laws preventing the rise of undue market power.

Monopolistic conditions are far more prevalent than we might think. Consider, for instance, the fact that a disproportionately large share of the United States is effectively serviced by only one health insurance provider.[6]

I recently experienced a minor example of monopoly in everyday life even though there are laws to protect us from it. I moved to a location that is only serviced by satellite television services. There are supposedly two different satellite service providers. However, when I began to look into the two services, I found that they were in lockstep. When one had a special offer, the other one did too. Base pricing was essentially the same, and the contractual terms were virtually identical. Oddly, no matter how hard I tried to contact a local installer of either of the services, I was always rerouted to a corporate office. When I did finally come across an installation service provider, I found that the vast majority of them offered installation for both of the satellite services. Under these conditions, how can we say that customers genuinely have a competitive alternative?

In this particular case, we have wandered well beyond anything that could be directly extracted from Scripture. At the same time, fundamental economic justice and fairness requires the prevention of unfair exploitation. And we cannot just passively expect people to "do the right thing." We need to create conditions that allow for a balance of power. In some cases, this can be created with proper attention to market forces. In other cases, it will be necessary for regulations to establish parameters.

Strengthening Families

Families are remarkably important. In fact, both the political left and right agree on the need to be proactive in its defense. There is a problem, however, with the vast majority of contemporary pro-family work. To put it simply, advocates for the family have taken the concept of the so-called "nuclear family"—a modernist construct—and elevated it above biblical concepts of the family. (Consider, for example, the size and extent of Abraham's family, which numbered over fifty people, including extended family and support.) This much more modernist conception narrows the sense of mutual responsibility required in Scripture. God expects us to live in communities of mutual interdependence—not just among members of nuclear families but among much broader senses of family, even our communities.

Unfortunately, the vast majority of our efforts to engage in policies that strengthen families quickly get entangled in partisan politics. That, in turn, too often results in misdirection and a failure to properly assess the challenges to the family. For example, the correlation between broken families and poverty is high. Yet the endless debate about which is cause and effect is unproductive. Instead, we need to begin to take concrete steps both to ease the stress on the family and to alleviate poverty. At the end of the day, we may never be able to move from correlation to causality, but the failure to be able to make this subtle distinction does not free us from the obligation to take constructive steps forward. For example, as we noted above, access to health care can be a remarkable strain on families with chronic health problems, and serious health care reform would be a powerful step toward strengthening families. Consider how strong families could be if we made a commitment to reduce child poverty by 50 percent in ten years and made sure that health care reform widely expanded health care access. A biblical vision of public life that pleases God must involve steps to alleviate poverty at all levels.

Global Poverty

The biblical injunction to put the interests of others over our own does not stop at our own national boundaries. These obligations are global in nature. For the purposes of our discussions, I am able to give only a cursory consideration to the issue of global poverty. While poverty is a serious problem in the United States (current figures put the poverty rate over 12 percent), there are many places in the world where poverty is far worse. Given that God blesses in order for us to bless others, Americans should shudder at the terrible obligations our wealth imposes on us.

It has been estimated that one-half of the world's population lives on the equivalent of less than $2.50 per day.[7] How will God judge wealthy Americans, who spend far more than that on eating out? We easily find justifications for not engaging the issue of global poverty more actively. ("We can't even address poverty at home. How can we be expected to alleviate global poverty?") Ultimately, however, all of our justifications are reducible to the fact that we enjoy our luxuries and do not want to give them up in order to meet the needs of the poor.

The Culture Wars: Homosexuality and Abortion

Without a doubt, the two most controversial issues at the intersection of faith and politics are homosexuality and abortion.

Neither issue is as simple as one might like to think, or as simple as either side represents it in their popular arguments. Let us take the concepts we have discussed throughout this book and see how we might lay out a position that balances the various concerns we have studied.

Homosexuality

References in Scripture to homosexuality are negative; when the subject comes up, Scripture denounces it.[8] Some biblical scholars provide plausible arguments that these scriptural references intend something other than monogamous homosexual relationships.[9] Others provide plausible arguments to the contrary. In the space we have, we will not be able to navigate these complex and highly contentious issues. Rather, let us recall that judging biblical intentions on particular behaviors should be limited by the way in which the behavior affects the common good. Even if we judge a particular behavior to be sinful, that does not mean that we should feel obliged to seek to outlaw that practice. There are plausible arguments to the claim that divorce is sinful. There might even be some evidence that it damages the common good. Few, however, argue for the criminalization of divorce. The freedom to make one's own decision on the question of divorce is greater than the downsides that divorce might cause.

Homosexuality falls into a similar category. Even if we cannot reach agreement on its moral status, individuals should be left free to make their own decisions about it. Homosexual people should not be discriminated against or denied basic rights and dignities. Little or no evidence exists that might suggest that the private behavior of gay and lesbian people harms the common good.

Fifty years from now we will know much more about the factors that give rise to homosexuality, and with that knowledge will come better ways to understand and address it. In the meantime, the most significant thing we as Christians can do is to participate in and encourage open and respectful dialogue between the alternative positions held by different parts of our culture. And we should make sure that gay and lesbian people are treated with the respect and love consistent with what Christians are called to grant to all persons.

Abortion

Few issues have proven to be more divisive across the political spectrum than abortion. Clinics have been bombed, doctors have been killed, and both sides refuse to compromise. For those who favor abortion rights, the issue is one of ensuring that women have rights over their own reproductive systems; for those who favor criminalizing abortion, the issue is one of protecting unborn children from premature death. One can see how the two sides can become so passionate on the issue. Let us see how we might assess abortion from both a public policy position and a Christian perspective.[10]

Despite creative exegesis and arguments to the contrary, Scripture does not explicitly address the question of abortion. However, as we have seen along the way, the fact that Scripture does not address an issue directly does not prevent us from drawing reasonable conclusions about it. There are many reasons to believe that the positions taken by both extremes—right and left—are problematic. On the one hand, the extreme that denies any justification for terminating a pregnancy overlooks too much. There are cases where the mother's health and even life is in jeopardy. Furthermore, the mental stresses that come with carrying a child conceived as a result of rape or incest are real. Are legislators, doctors, or pastors better positioned to help women make decisions about abortion in these cases?

At the other end of the spectrum are those who hold that abortion is a birth control option of last resort. However, even if we have legitimate debates about when life begins, should we not err on the side of caution? Within the bounds of the health of the mother, we should exercise restraint in ending a pregnancy when we cannot definitively resolve the question of the beginning of life. In other words, we should do as much as we can (some would say short of jailing mothers and doctors) to protect human life. Too easily we allow ourselves to be drawn into interminable debates about which side is right, but there is an alternative we can take.

A number of steps have been shown to be effective in reducing the perceived need for abortions. From a Christian perspective, our goal should not be an ideological position for or against but rather a pragmatic position that actually results in abortion reduction. For example, abortions could be significantly decreased if a number of basic medical services were available to lower-income women. Examples include contraceptives for those on Medicaid, medical coverage for pregnant women (for health care and hospital care), and day care for infants after birth. Frequently, economic factors become decisive in the decision to get an abortion. Steps such as these provide the basic support mechanisms that demonstrably reduce the perceived need for abortion and, thus, the actual number of abortions. At the very least we should argue for legislation that makes sure that women have access to support. Should additional steps be taken to prevent certain types of abortion procedures? This would be appropriate, but while we work out the proper protections for both women and the unborn we should move on those steps we know are helpful.

The Guttmacher Institute has found that the decriminalization of abortions often results in an initial increase in the number of abortion procedures.[11] However, in the long term, abortion rates generally drop. I have spoken with politically conservative doctors who do not favor the criminalization of abortion because they have seen too many women suffer the consequences of "back alley" abortions. They want to see the number of abortions reduced, but do not see criminalization as the best way to get the desired outcome. Undoubtedly this issue will remain at the fore of the "culture wars" for some time, but Christians should be committed to cooperating in order to significantly identify ways to reduce the number of abortions.

Conclusions

It would be easy to extend our discussions far beyond where we have taken them so far, but that would take us beyond an attempt to simply open a dialogue. I have not spent a good deal of time citing studies that warrant the claims I have made because my goal is not to "prove" that particular methods are the ones that we must follow. Rather, I have given examples of the kinds of policies and programs that might yield the sorts of outcomes necessary to empower the way of being and living together that God intends for us. My own theopolitical position is that I tend to be right of center theologically and left of center politically. The kinds of policies and programs I have outlined here tend to arise from that theopolitical position. I would be delighted to see people from different theopolitical positions take up this set of issues and offer their own perspectives. This could begin a healthy and productive discussion that might allow us as Christians to develop and articulate a range of positions that would empower the way of living together that pleases God. Then we could begin to see these different proposals piloted and tested in different geographical locations with the goal of actually determining which ones best enable the life that pleases God. What a marvelous move beyond the almost immediate descent into ideology and partisan politics that so often characterizes our public discourse on these issues!

As we have argued throughout, trying to identify the biblical role of government is the wrong place to start. Rather, we must begin our inquiry by trying to discern the general contours of how God intends for us to live together. Of course, the answer to that question is not one that can be answered by appealing to a handful of popular biblical texts. There are numerous reasons why this approach is inadequate and will likely lead us to faulty conclusions. Instead, we must seek to develop an understanding of what would constitute a biblical view of community—what do communities (local, national, international) that please God look like? To discern this, we examined a wide range of texts from both the Old and New Testaments. Only after that were we able to begin to reflect on the appropriate roles for both public and private sectors. Since our discussion has dealt primarily with the public sector, we have not attempted to flesh out the details of the appropriate place for private institutions except to note that we cannot afford to omit them. Our broader goal has been to consider the role that public policies and institutions might play in empowering life together as God intends, and we have found that numerous existing policies and programs do, in fact, serve that end. In this last section, we briefly examined a host of public policies in attempt to see how different biblical expectations for our shared life might be served. Other policies might exist, and possibly even better ones for accomplishing the goals we identified from our study of Scripture. Consequently, this book has been more of an exercise in attempting to "think Christianly" about public institutions and their role in developing communities that live out God's intentions. It has been much less concerned with trying to prove that my own political and theological positions are the only ones likely to work. As Christians, we should be less motivated by our own presuppositions and ideological commitments, and increasingly driven to determine pragmatically what will actually empower the life that pleases God. Consider this an invitation to dialogue and a springboard for further discussion as we strive together not only to think Christianly but also to live Christianly at all levels of our societies.

Notes

Chapter 1 Introduction

1. Jim Wallis, *God's Politics: Why the Right Gets It Wrong and the Left Doesn't Get It* (San Francisco: HarperOne, 2005).

2. We do not have space for lengthy critique of the false dichotomies that pigeonhole people into either the "right" or the "left." Suffice it to say that theopolitical positions are much more complex.

3. Of course, Christians have an impact on society beyond their involvement in government. They have an even more significant role through the church, for example. In this book, we assume this, but look specifically at how Christians should be involved in and affect government.

4. Consider, for example, his *The Second Coming of the Church* (Nashville: Word, 1998).

5. Steve Chake is a social activist and author with his home base in the UK. He is an ordained Baptist minister and the founder of Oasis Trust. Find out more about him at http://mmpublicrelations.com/page.php?page=project&intID=105&intParentID=3.

6. Cal Thomas and Ed Dobson, *Blinded by Might: Why the Religious Right Can't Save America* (Grand Rapids: Zondervan, 2000).

7. An advertising campaign by Sojourners. For more details, see http://www.Sojo.net.

Chapter 2 Reading Scripture

1. John Howard Yoder, *For the Nations: Essays Evangelical and Public* (Grand Rapids: Eerdmans, 1997), 24; emphasis mine.

2. N. T. Wright, *The Challenge of Jesus* (Downers Grove, IL: InterVarsity, 1999), 27, 51.

3. One might consider *The Drama of Scripture* by Michael Goheen and Craig Bartholomew (Grand Rapids: Baker Academic, 2004).

4. Rikki E. Watts, *Isaiah's New Exodus in Mark* (Grand Rapids: Baker Academic, 2000).

Chapter 3 The God of Abraham, Isaac, Jacob, and Jesus

1. See, for example, Friedrich Nietzsche, *Thus Spake Zarathustra: A Book for Everyone and No One*, trans. R. J. Hollingsdale (New York: Penguin, 1961), 160.

2. For more information see http://www.CurtCloninger.com/shows.

3. Roland H. Bainton, *Here I Stand: A Life of Martin Luther* (Peabody, MA: Hendrickson, 1950).

4. See, for example, Paul Tillich, *Systematic Theology* (Chicago: University of Chicago Press, 1957), 2:14.

5. See Gregory of Nyssa, *On "Not Three Gods,"* http://www.newadvent.org /fathers/2905.htm.

6. E.g., Wright, *Challenge of Jesus*, 76.

Chapter 4 Biblical Vignettes

1. See Yoder, *For the Nations*.

2. See John Locke, *Two Treatises on Government and a Letter Concerning Toleration* (1688; New Haven: Yale University Press, 2003), 28.210.

3. See Yoder, *For the Nations*, 63–64.

4. This is not, of course, to deny that God can work his agenda in the midst of unjust legislation. He can. However, the fact that God can turn stones into bread does not relieve our responsibilities to feed the poor. Our obligation to create just societal structures is rooted in who we are to be, not in a lack of confidence in God's power.

5. From Martin Luther's preface to the book of James in the first edition of his German New Testament.

6. Dietrich Bonhoeffer, *The Cost of Discipleship*, trans. R. H. Fuller and Irmgard Booth (New York: Touchstone, 1995).

7. Patrick Miller, *Deuteronomy*, Interpretation (Louisville: John Knox, 1990), 138.

8. Economies redistribute wealth; that, quite simply, is what they do. The question is whether they will redistribute it justly.

Chapter 5 Human Governance and the Kingdom Agenda

1. See, for example, N. T. Wright, *Jesus and the Victory of God* (Minneapolis: Fortress, 1996), 151.

2. William T. Cavanaugh, *Theopolitical Imagination: Christian Practices of Space and Time* (London: T&T Clark, 2003), 9.

3. For example, while moral rights and wrongs about sexual expression are found in Scripture, we need not have laws legislating the sexual practices of consenting adults.

4. Stefan Zweig, *The Right to Heresy: Castiello against Calvin*, trans. Eden and Cedar Paul (New York: Viking, 1936).

5. Zweig's work focuses on the burning of Michael Servetus at the stake over his Christology. Was he a heretic? Perhaps. Should he have been burned over it? It is hard to see the justification.

6. See Tony Campolo, *Red Letter Christians: A Citizen's Guide to Faith and Politics* (Ventura, CA: Regal, 2008).

7. Stanley Hauerwas and William H. Willimon, *Resident Aliens: Life in the Christian Colony* (Nashville: Abingdon, 1989), 94.

Chapter 6 Public Policy and the Kingdom Agenda

1. Consider *Leviathan* by Thomas Hobbes (1651; Oxford: Oxford University Press, 1996) or *On the Social Contract* by Jean-Jacques Rousseau (1762; Indianapolis: Hackett, 1987).

2. Data can be examined at "Social Security Reduces Elderly Poverty," The Social Security Network, http://www.socsec.org/feature.asp?issueid ={0A45711A-0BF9-46D2-A74E-F47450A624E4}.

3. As is often the case, the percentages were even worse for minority groups. Trends over the last ten years suggest that this number will continue to rise.

4. Madison Park, "45,000 American Deaths Associated with Lack of Insurance," CNNHealth.com, September 18, 2009, http://www.cnn.com/2009 /HEALTH/09/18/deaths.health.insurance.

5. Consider Exodus 22:24–25, Psalm 15, and Proverbs 28:8, for example.

6. See the article from the American Medical Association at http://www .ama-assn.org/ama1/pub/upload/mm/368/compstudy_52006.pdf.

7. See http://www.globalissues.org/article/26/poverty-facts-and-stats.

8. Some make an important distinction between *being homosexual* and *engaging in homosexual practice.* For those who make this distinction, the latter is problematic but the former is not.

9. I use the term *plausible*, but I resist entering the argument about the validity of these arguments. Merely plausible arguments can be true or false. I will leave the specific question of which side is right to others. We are more focused on how Christians might forge reasonable public policy that is consistent with their beliefs and commitments.

10. Sadly, our "start-the-conversation" approach will prevent an analysis of the underlying question, and that, undoubtedly, will leave both sides dissatisfied. I encourage each to undertake a serious study of the positions of the other side and open dialogue, resisting the urge to allow the discussion to immediately collapse into namecalling and recriminations.

11. See "Trends in the Characteristics of Women Obtaining Abortions, 1974 to 2004," Guttmacher Institute, August 2008, http://www.guttmacher.org/pubs/2008/09/23/TrendsWomenAbortions-wTables.pdf.

Index

Made in the USA
Middletown, DE
22 September 2016